THE MYSTIC

AND

OTHER POEMS,

BY

PHILIP JAMES BAILEY,

AUTHOR OF "FESTUS."

BOSTON:

TICKNOR AND FIELDS.

M DCCC LVI.

AUTHOR'S EDITION.

CAMBRIDGE:
STEREOTYPED AND PRINTED BY METCALF AND COMPANY.

CONTENTS.

THE MYSTIC.

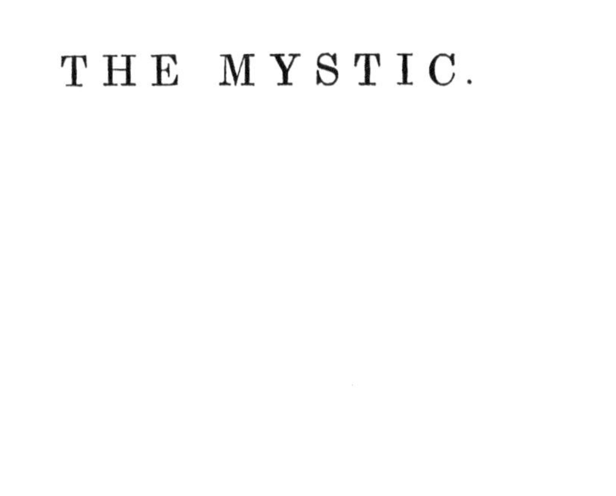

THE MYSTIC.

Who holds not life more yearful than the hours
Since first into this world he wept his way,
Erreth much, may be. Called of God, man's soul
In patriarchal periods, comet-like,
Ranges perchance all spheres successive; and in each,
With nobler powers endowed and senses new,
Set season bideth. So with him it seemed
Of whom I speak, the initiate of the light,
The adopted of the water and the sun.

Time's sand-dry streamlet through its glassy straits
Flowed ceaseless; and he lived a threefold life
Through all the ages; yea, seven times his soul
Commingling, leavened with its light the world.
First in the feasts of life, and the sun's son,
Through all God's homely universe he roamed

Lordly, and spake to earth the lore of stars,
The mother-tongue of Heaven our Fatherland.
Born to instate mankind in veriest truths,
By nature symbolled in gem, bloom, and wing;
To give to all the hope of bliss reserved,
And ultimate certainty of angelhood,
He, like a river which through gullies, rocks,
And deserts runs its purifying race
To Ocean's thrice regenerative depths,
Chose thorough all probations his own path,
And voluntary trode the downward way;
For they whose eyen by spirit-fire are purged
Move ever up the reascent to light,
On a cœlestial gradient, paved with wings;
Disrobed him of all privilege, and alone
Suffered the dignities yearned for by the mass
But that he might ennoble servitude.

Grounded in Nature's sacred cipher, he
The myth-insculptured language of the light,
In templed tome and lay columnar read,
The masque of gods. But not all spirits can bear,
Untutored, full and free access of truth.
The sage, who ken the verities of soul,
Whose be the preview clear of prophet-bard

To ope the inner spirit by outward keys,
Who while unclothing still can screen the truth,
That inexpressive wisdom — silence known —
Unless in this wise, lip them not aloud.

Initiate and perfect in mysteries,
He graduated triumphant. Thrice he set
His foot upon the mount of light divine
And eyed the all beneath him. First, ere earth,
Like the libation of a crownéd bowl,
O'erspilled the depths of the unknown abyss,
By Nile with honey flowing, that through soil
Promethean, swift as eagle pouncing, drops
Oceanwards, sun-beloved and primal land
Of magic marvels; giant head of earth
First looming from the flinty seed of fire
And pre-æternal darkness — eldest ally
Of lost Atlantis, lost ere Europe crept
From Chaos' lap, — long time he wandered; (him
His mother, child of royal priest, conceived
Dreaming of Gods in visions of the night,
Amid consphærate harmonies, and awaked
Never until she clasped her dream-born;) bent
To snatch from labyrinthine secrecies,
Wherein the holy mystics taught their rites,

Regenerant Truth; from hall to hall pursue,
As though from sphere to sphere the winged soul,
Through all disguise the æternal unity;
Through all terrestrial ill cœlestial good;
Through triple darkness light; through matter's marble veil
The divine spirit, all parent of the sun,
Queen of heaven's azure world-hive, celled with stars.

He at his birth the starry stamps received,
For every limb held commune with its god,
And planetary gifts plenipotent;
The moon dispensed him riches, and the sun
Mind-wealth, that so before his dazéd eyne
The splendid spectrum of immortal fame
Perpetual danced; soul-compulsory power,
The god of psychopompous function, round
Circling the sun with fourfold force; love's star
The joys that come with beauteous shapes and eyes
Dewy and blue; courage the god-star red;
Supremacy and justice they who held
Successive, if usurped sway, o'er the skies.

Around him lay the great concerted whole;
The moaning winds and cadent waters, fire

Aspirant, sea bass-toned and reboant earth;
For only man's crude ear of discord dreams,
Jarring the orbéd harmonies of heaven.
And for the cause that soon as born his lips
Dropped music, like to the dew-bright beads of honey
From fleshy flowerets pendent, nectarous, he
The over-dominant movement of all life
Knew, and elicited its vital moods.

The soul of every animal, from the ox,
Thunder begotten, to the solar wolf—
As he re-rose from Hades,—god of death,
Thenceforward to man hallowed—to destroy
The spirit of all ill; and scarab, type
Of the great world-artificer; from the lord
Of golden flocks, lamb-headed, to the goat
Sacred to sin in all rites, he, in turn,
Bespake, and each to him the awful word
Passed, that makes ope the thousand courts of life;
The universal and æternal sign,
Itself life, death and immortality,
Which silenceth yet answereth all demands,
And bindeth evil with an endless chain.
Armed and impowered therewith, no foe he fears
Who seeks salvation in the heights of heaven.

Asp-crowned, gold shod (thus treat the abhorréd gold
Of false esteem), his breast bedight with gems,—
Home of all virtues and the embrace of Truth,—
He prayed, he prophesied, divined, and judged.

In granite graven, and on porphyry hall,
And ceiling, with imperishable touch,
He wrought the rise of night, and chaos' growth,
The gross alluvium of time's turbid stream,—
And birth of Love, that venerable babe,
The recreator he of deathless life;
Wrought in that spirit awe-bound, wherewith, of old,
The workman chiselled some cherubic shape,
Nor knew but that the God who doth create
And animate the whole—from whom the whole,
Like essenced, emanateth—might appear
In manifestive brightness, and array
His Being in the form the holy artist framed.

Close dogged by evil he the dateless hills,
Mountains of gems, of gold, of silver gained,
Within whose wombs he wonned; but chased in vain;
For the more vanquished he, more power was his.
Him, naked ghosts of maddening beauty, lamped
By green and glistering gryphons' lidless eyes,

Led to alchemic vaults, where sat some seer
Great jewels minting, and from the refuse gold,
That naught be wasted, rounding royal crowns.
The costliest of all treasures, knowledge how
Like treasures to produce, he gathered there,
Nor cumbered him with perishable proofs.
Though by this tempted, and that warned, he took
The path of light, instinctive, and was saved.
For having fought his way through flood and flame,
Helped by good dæmons, hindered by the bad,
And closed the gates of thunder on the gods
Where they in their marmoreal heaven abode,
Dark as the hourless mansions of the dead,
And tested all things; in the coffined core
Of the heaven-wedding pyramid, at last
He fainted in perfection; and discerned
How sweet was truth, for death in truth was life.

In that blest death the gods divided him,
And the stars claimed the portions erst their own;
They so adored him. World-beloved was he.
The sun his head; the starry souls his eyes;
His locks redundant asked the watery powers;
The living spirit his temples; his strong hand
The lord of fate; his bent knee worshipful

The goddess of divine life; and his feet
The guardian of the destinies of souls.

Dear to the bearded serpent, spirit supreme,
Whose omnipresent eye approves the world,—
Eye of the world of life, and nature's soul,
Who lapped him in his cold blue coils, and flew
Where live the stars: there, 'mid nocturnal day
Where Death's grim orb illumes the restless ghosts,
And with his scourge on their own hearts inscribes
The tortures of the evils they have done,
He, weighed 'gainst Truth, down-dipped the skyey scale.

Thence, hawk-like, through the purgatorial air,
And many-regioned æther, peaceful, pure,
Soul-quickening, soared he to the crescent moon,
And sailed the sky's abysmal sea of suns
In ark crystalline, manned by beamy gods,
To drag the deeps of space, and net the stars,
Where, in their nebulous shoals, they shore the void,
And, through old night's Typhonian blindness, shine.
Then, solarized, he pressed onwards to the sun,
Lord of the living, guardian of all good;
And, in the heavenly Hades, hall of God,—
Whose eye begat the sun, whose mind the moon,

The goodness and the wisdom of their sire, —
Had final welcome of the firmament.
The true, triunal God, thrice-greatest, one,
Man, man-god, God, who symbolled, led him through
The sky-arched, God-built temple of the world.

TIME's arid rivulet through its glassy gorge
Lapsed ceaseless; and again by Gunga's wave,
(O life and bliss assuring fount of heaven,
The life-flowings divine of Deity,
How mighty, how mysterious is thy name!)
He, of a damsel, sacred to the god,
With fellow-maidens sporting, whom a cloud
Of sunset glory clasped, and circumfused
With vital brilliance, dropping—next was born.

Through the star-gates of the high luminous land
Came down the immortal aspirant of life.
With royal abnegation of all power
Prior, all motion, many a million years
He had suffered as a mountain, and to heaven,
In fiery heart-floods, for a thousand moons
Without pause, preconfessed his sins, and then
Æternal silence laid her snow-cold hand
Upon his lips, and they were iced for ever;

(After in life, the mount wherein he had been
Enstoned he recognized, and felt it throb
Beneath his footsteps, heartlike 'neath a hand.)
A thousand years, an oak, he crowned the hill,
And navies traced to him their ancestry;
In the sea's arms a million suns he passed;
Among the insect race that winged the air
Or crawl the dust, the like; among the birds
That skim the sky, a myriad; thrice that term
Through all four-footed tribes of nature, fierce
Or bland; from these, through various grades of men,
Of divers nations the o'er-topping stems,
To the high peers of perfect sanctity,
Native wherein, at length, the hundredth time,
By pure persistency in sacred rites,
And stern assimilations of the soul
To fleshless life, even as the holy live,
Through seven bright spheres successive, he, his soul
Lift upwards, like a mountain by the main,
That laves his marble feet sea-deep, and high
O'er shore, plain, verdure, cloud, snow, vapor, bares
To the chill sky his reverent brow; and he
This our initial world where all things fixed
Or free are passed; the re-existent orb
Skyey wherein, until time's destined doom,

All that have lived mindful of sacrifice
And holy rites sleep calm; and, as he passed,
He to the dimly gleaming shadows taught
A prayer would ring them entrance into bliss,
Like to the magic horn, in faerie halls,
Of blast resistless; thrice blown, every gate
Of every palace opens like a flower:
The odorous home of lightness, coolness, warmth,
Change pleasing and perpetual, where they bide,
Imbowered in all delights conceivable,
Who, perfected by God's love to themselves,
And that pure love to all His love requires,
Upsoar to heaven, immediate, as the soul
Bursts from its bodily chrysalis; — the mid-world
Between celestial and terrestrial spheres,
Where first the denizens of each commune,
Without or veil or shadow, toil or mask;
There giants and divinities divide
The far-expanded sphere, and now in peace,
But oftener far in war; the birth-world where
The souls of the unhallowed, of all creeds
And nations, dwell; where lower lives, too, lost
For sins of man, by general doom of fire,
Or flood, or sacrifice, are all re-born; —
The mansion of the penitent blessed, where saints

Austere, and sons of the Supreme, self-ruled,
Reside in infinite freedom, to which sphere
A silver gate, a golden to the last,
Gives access; the abode sublime of truth;
By wisdom, duty, verity only gained,
Gained never to be lost; for there is God,
Creator, and Preserver, and Destroyer;
Initial, and perfection of all Being;
The infinite fulness of all spirit; sum
And sun of all the souls of all the spheres,
Wherein, through every life of man or brute, —
In origin, not end, alike divine, —
He darts his raylets vital and æterne,
He, the untempled God, above man's thought.

For lo! time's end, when, on his snowy steed,
The great Preserver, blazing like some star,
That with dischevelled infinites of light
Between the sun's breast and the icy arms
Of space extremest oscillates, sudden draws,
From out its sheathéd night, his gleaming glaive,
And robs the age of life; then, all renewed,
Peace, innocence, and purity shall bind
In flowery chains, the bonds of liberty,
The race divine of man, the fruit of God; —

And the whole earth, though now half-burning sands
Or frost-white wilds, bloom into Paradise.
And after, even this shall cease ; the spirit,
Inured to meditate alone on God,
Pleasure no more can please, finds scant delight
In fragrant fields, grows discontent with heaven ;
Yea, in pure wantonness with terror, tears
The masque material from Time's phantom face.
All Being shall then be reabsorbed in God,
All minor deities in Him shall merge,
As water vases, broken in mid-sea,
Unite therewith the element they contained,
And add their calculable drops to its
Immensurable abysses, whence were cast,
As out of moulds, the mountains of the world ;
For all that shows not God, illusion is.

And as earth's thousand seas, streams, lakelets, pools,
Their separate image of the star of noon
Hold, though he be but one, so every soul
Its semblance of the One Divine retains
Which all illumines, sweetens all ; and his,
Affied to God, in massive ease and power
Languescent, well might wield the world at will
Whose whispered mandates awed the thunder down.

He, lion-like within the desert, dwelled
From men apart, and so, intact of soul,
In heart ascetic, continent in thought,
The intelligible luxuries of life
Shunned; to a boundless level planed his soul;
Fasted on fruits; and out of writhen frond,
Or flowery chalice, quaffed the fountain free.

By virtue of which liberated state,
Lofty and passionless as date-palm's bride,
High on the upmost summits of his soul,
Wrought of the elemental light of heaven,
And pure and plastic flame that soul could show,
Whose nature, like the perfume of a flower
Enriched with aromatic sun-dust, charms
All, and with all ingratiates itself,
Sat dazzling purity; for loftiest things,
Snow-like, are purest. As in mountain morns
Expectant air the sun-birth, so his soul
Her God into its supra-natural depths
Accepted brightly and sublimely. Vowed
To mystic visions of supernal things;
Daily endowed with spheres and astral thrones,
His, by pre-emptive right, throughout all time;
Immerged in his own essence, clarified

From all those rude propensities which rule
Man's heart, a tyrant mob, and, venal, sell
All virtues, aye the crown of life to what
Passion soe'er præpotent, worst deludes
Or deftliest flatters, he, death-calm, beheld,
As though through glass of some far-sighting tube,
The restful future; and, consummed in bliss,
In vital and æthereal thought abstract,
The depths of Deity and heights of heaven.

Attached to things divine alone, as seal
To chart affixed, he all truth taught and sought,
Sweetly retired. As Eden's olive groves,
That, in the luminous mysteries of the sun
Perfectly ripened, were withdrawn to heaven
So pure, and so intact, like diamond gas
Exhaling 'neath the keen, fire-hearted lens,
Lighter than light, imponderable power,
His spirit soared, unwavering, up the skies.
He to the deities, as his nearer blood,
Willed all his grand domains, in trust, to keep
Holy and free; and still, to bar all strife,
His poor and ignorant kin, the kings of earth,
He piteously remembered ere he passed
Through deathland, to the ultimate realm of light,

And shared his orts among them; they, his gates
Quitting, scarce grumbled their ungrateful thanks,
Because that, like the setting sun, he left
A world of gold behind him, free to all.

TIME's arid streamlet through its glassy gorge
Flowed pauseless; and, by Sida's crystal flood,
Which, as with sea seven-tided, bathes the base
Of the high mount of vision, he was born
Again, to teach, to all the nations, life.

Born of the tree blood-sapped, which, on the steep
Of knowledge, thrice, by vital wind, impregned,
Buds forth her life, the mother of the world,
Upon the royal rock four-faced, he dwelled,
The tripod mountain, with its jewelled feet
Long while; the orient side of silver pure;
Beryl, the brow which overawes the sun,
When, abdicating Heaven, he calls the stars
To attest his end imperial; the dead north
Of glowing gold, the south of ruby paled.

Up shining streams and over odorous lakes,
In golden boat or silver, pearly oared,
Dimpling the wave, he sped; or dashing high

The fragrant foam; and now his limbs imbathed
Amid immortal nymphs, serenely pure,
Like living lilies floating on the tide,
In love with their own shadows, as they lay
Beneath the cooling moon. From sacred trees
Ambrosial fruit and gem-wrought raiment, tinct
With the sun's infinite aureole, he culled;
And walked resplendent with his meteor eyes
Thrice round the dragon king, world-lifed, who saw
The first, and will the last of gods surview;
So vast and vile a monster, heaven and earth
With thunderous groans and lurid blushes hid
Their starry heads, when God, in words of fire,
Asked them his generation, — Hell-begot,
Hell-born, they said, we know no more of him.
Yet sought he not illumination thence,
But due confession of divinity;
For, in the radiance of a frame divine,
In natal and cœlestial light he stood.

Though pure in aspiration, pure as is
The pearl-rose halo round a star, so, proof
Of the divine within us and the strain
Of the cœlestial heavenward, yet he sinned,
In virtue of his nature, and sought earth;

For sin is nature; and through all life's gates,
Like to the perishing flowery arches reared
Before some fane, he willed to pass, for he
The ultimate sanctity and æternal joy
Foreknew that they led up to; and, perchance,
By his own consciousness of final bliss,
He might the hearts of millions fortify.

Now the destruction and re-birth of things
He saw, and preached, and warned mankind they came;
By water first; the gentlest rain distils
In the beginning like small dust, until,
Enlarging, gradual, every drop descends
Huge as a millstone, and all life is drowned;
Then rise seven suns, successive, and at once
Inhabit Heaven, till the whole orb be drained
Of ocean, sea, lake, river, moisture, damp,
Parched to a powder; last of all, a wind
Light as a leaf's breath 'gins to blow, and blows
Stronger and stronger, till the tempestuous blast
Uproots the mountains, eddying them about
Like feathers in a whirlpool; all the rocks,
Disintegrate, lie loose and level dust,
And the vast sphere is scattered o'er the skies,
Like sand o'er an arena. Water again

Installs the regeneration of the world,
Condensing some few atoms which the wind
Rounds into rain-drops; and, cohæring thus,
Drives languidly together, mass by mass;
The lighter particles rise, and air become;
The grosser fall, and cause the element earth;
This, fire solidifies, till, whole at length,
The fused orb rehabilitated rolls
As theretofore upon its cœlar path.
Thus, thrice made pure, by water, fire, and wind,
In essence, earth spreads wide her lap, and heaven
(In flowery showers, cropped by the hand of gods,
Fruits, riches, and the robes of truth) descends;
While censer-clouds condensed of sun-fired fragrancies
Perfect the sweet lustration of all life.

In saintly destitution, sacred need,
He, light of time, his life-day harmless passed,
Sparing all life by charity; and, since
All soul-sin seems a missing of the mark
Resultant from imperfect force or aim,
Exhorting all to look and work for good,
In the supreme beneficence of God.
For evil is temporal only, nor can be
In the divine æternal. From the void,

Along with bright creation, as its shade,
It rose, and back to vasty void returns.

Time's arid runnel through its glassy gorge
Glode ceaseless ; and, anon, where the huge stream,
Son of the sea, bursts through the skyey gates,
Born of an angel maid and heaven descended,
Who, bathing in its midst, the white-orbed flower,
Of root eternal born, eternal bud,
Upon its waters floating, tasted and ate ;
Till, her within, its golden-dusted stem
Branched crosswise into life, and fructified
To soul ; the flower-begotten son of heaven,
From birth immediate, perfected his steps,
Assuming all divinity ; and hailed
Himself the incorporate order of the skies.

Nursed by the starry sea and those twin lakes
Named eyes of heaven, and fed on the bright gems
Dropped from dracontian lips, whose virtue gave
Sole sustenance to his being, and whereby
The living lines, on fiery wivern's back,
The secret counsel of the universe
Once read, translated all things, he achieved
At one enlightening pang and blessed his woe.

Reason supreme him made innately wise,
The stars prophetic and the holy moon,
Interpreter to time of things æterne,
Ruler of rites and sacred festivals.

And the invisible heavens the giant world
Through him instructed; him, O star of earth!
Thou saddest, wisest, eldest of all lights!
The formless origin of things, and how,
Proceeding from itself, the infinite
Finite becomes; returning thitherward,
The finite infinite, whereby the parts,
O'erleaping the interstitial net of death,
Regain that continuity of soul
Which ones them with the boundless and divine.

Throned upon lion hides and dragon skins, —
Cloud-breathing dragons homed in heights of air,
Amid the golden land his mellower years,
Studious of immortality, he passed; —
Now by the moon-enclosing mountain, now
Scaling the cloud-throne where the immortal fowl
Of mighty fortune wafts from his jewelled nest
The winds of all the world, — he gave the youth
Ubiquitous dominion 'tween his wings;

And bore him swift to the cities of the skies,
Gleaming aloft, tranquil, in starry bliss; —
Now where the sacred soul-tree scents the breeze,
'Mid marble cities, by the shore of pearl;
Or where the fountain, sprung from lightning flash,
The fire-born water, flows, in whose bright depths
He consecrates himself; around its source
The true immortals dwell, of man unseen.

Where, on the hill of dreams, the flower of sleep
Flings forth its silky leaflets, he the juice
Drank of millennial herb, a thousand years
All blight resisting, which to age brings back
Electric youth, the glory, this, of earth,
And king of flowers. From him the holy learned
Religion, justice, temperance, wisdom, faith,
Outer and inner knowledge, endogenous truth,
The five-fold world and elemental lore;
All mysteries hidden and imperfect, all
Public and perfect secrets of the world,
Of Heaven, earth, lightning, mountains, fire, and clouds,
Water and wind, and when the end draws nigh.
To spirit transcendent of inferior spheres
Nature is always ominous; notes of birds
Doomful, and animal movements; sun-shot gleams,

And noon-day apparitions, shades, and pools
Wherein the eve-star tricks her tresses bright;
And upward arts of fire; presaging all
Immortal destinations that so man,
In likeness of divine perfection made,
Happy on earth but happier far on high,
Might reinstall the primal state of heaven.

Alms gave he, as an alchemist, whose gold
Flows inexhaustless, or whose pearly draught
The potable perpetuity of life
Vouched to its proud possessor; till at last
As man, the errant babe, intent on death,
In orbital aphelion with his sire,
Back to the irresistible bosom of love
Wheels his precipitous foot, and with a smile,
Foreseeing his apotheosis there,
Bounds to embrace the beauty infinite;
So he, divinely rooted in the world,
And lifting into life his facial flower,
Back to the pre-eternals called of God,
Passed, disappearing in the essential heavens.

TIME's sand-dry runnel through its glassy strait
Flowed checkless; and the immortal seeker now,

The son of seven bright parents, orbs divine
In precreative fire conjunctive ranged,
Upon the hallowed ground where Phrat still pours
His Paradeisal wavelets, cave-born, stood,
Gray-bearded from his birth; and onward, urged
By the divine affinities of truth,
Which, in the lowest depth, sees but a step
Back to the pure perfection of the heavens,
He crept, in stifling darkness, through a cave
High vaulted, yea a world cave, where, as in Heaven,
The truth first glimmered on him like a star;
Showing where waited him a white winged steed,
That, fed on fiery adders, slaked his throat
From burning wells. Him mounting, on he sped
Through lions, wolves, and dragons, men of might,
Open or secret enemies, sands of fire
And storms of hail, the world's contempt or hate,
The spells of wine and gold, luxurious love,
Seductive beldames and adulterous ghouls,
Vices that flesh devour, defile the dead,
The sun-fowl, spirit of life-consuming time,
The dæmons that in mental darkness dwell,
The brazen fort of royal tyranny,
With sin-black hills engirthed (circumferent six,
Central the seventh) all-mastering, though half-spent;

Through threatening files of flamy ghosts and fiends
Created from primæval darknesses;
The horrors of all visionary hells;
Huge spectral dæmons, figurative of sins;
And clueless mazes to the mouldy abyss
Where, couched on rottenness, and guarded sole
By pitfalls brimmed with crawling, weltering worms,
Lo! the white monster which appalls the world;
Death, but not him. O'er moats of sanguine slime,
And towers where glared a green and ghastly light,
And battlemented walls of human bones,
He sprang triumphant on his shrieking foe;
Smote him, and from his heart three blood-drops black —
Black as the night the Son-God passed in hell —
Wrung; thence ascending by a starry stair,
Each step a bliss, a virtue, he emerged
Soldier of God, and conqueror of all fear,
Therewith to purge the eye of wisest man.

Scaling on foot the mount of heavenly fire,
Where throned on triple columns sate the sun,
He, in the glory of the bridegroom, stood,
And knelt to hear the luminaries divine,
The first created witnesses of God,
Who in His bosom holds the living world

As shepherd in his arms star-spotted fawn.
From the moon's hand her starry stole he took,
And zonelet studded with thrice ten beamy rings,
Shining with light genetic, either side
Broidered with signs, though breathing, living not.
Indued, bespake him then the Perfect Light
In wisdom's signal silence, and unrolled
Before his eyes the archives of the heavens,
The original deeds of God's great government,
Star-writ, the golden-winged tongue of gods,
Time's charter, and the fire-bound book of love,
And heaven's all trinal lights. There too he viewed,
Participator of God's general light,
The infinite circlet filled of Deity,
The world-wheel through the which he had winged in soul
Beyond the high and azure plain of truth,
To alight upon the peak of happiness: —
There converse held with all the eloquent orbs,
Interpretative stars, and counselling gods,
Who thoughts divine, thoughts earthly, interchange.

Sword, sceptre, key were given him, robe of white,
And ring of royalty, wherewith he found
Due worship of the golden-bearded kings,

Who from the mystic satchel where the lots
Are cast of destiny, to him brought forth
The inedible fruit of immortality.
They in his hands the volumed lightnings laid,
And bound him by an oath which all things heard,
In thunderous echo of the unuttered word.
The balanced hemispheres he held, wherein
The good and evil of all time are weighed,
With universal justice, whence is shown,
By all-solicitous love and doom divine,
Man is, of God, the mean, and God, man's end;
For to the true soul all are ends divined,
From everlasting, to their ordinal stand.

Out of the world-bright cup of divination,
Filled from the stream of life, that 'neath the throne
Of light rolls ever, where its rhythmic flow
Breaks into song-fraught wavelets lipped with light,
He quaffed, and, mirrored in its rim, beheld
All forms of future things; the magic rose,
Of speechless virtue, proof 'gainst all vile charms,
That blossomed on the bank, he culled and smelled,
And, from its fragrance, knowledge of the passed
Perfumed his being; from the whole he knew,
Truth of all times and wisdom of all worlds,

3

That all the constellations of the skies
Shall lapse into the lamb, within his arms
The cross of light upreared, while in her hand
The virgin tunes her star-strung, lilied lyre.

Of the cœlestial vine, ten thousand branched,
Which stretcheth o'er the skyey roof of earth,
Heaven's holy tree, whereon the luminous fruit
Of soul unborn, in glittering clusters hung,
One by one dropping into mortal moulds,
A golden shower, he tasted; and by stealth
Plucked from the pomegranates of Paradise,
Unknown to crowds, the secret fruit of life,
Star-orbed, immortal, ripe with solar seed
The single seed, deathful yet mastering death,
And knew himself divinified; for he,
With lote and holy honeysuckle crowned,
As well the bruised theangeline, which gives
Prophetic sense, as juice of aglaophant,
That subjects to the eye the invisible world,
And hom sweet herblet of immortal life,
Sipped, till transmute he stood, star-headed; felt
His eyes irradiate with an inward light,
And recognized his angels where they wheeled,
Like mated falcons round their creanced young,

Saluting him in rapture, man of men,
Sole son of life, the crown and heir of time.

They with him ranged the lucent orb throughout
In after times man's home to be, wherein
Plain, perfect, shadowless, like a globe of glass,
Men shall be known of separate nations only
Because their lands of different jewels are;
The continents of diamond, isles of pearl;
There shall be but two mountains, this of gold,
Of silver that; the seas shall all be wine,
The lakelets hydromel, the rivers milk;
And, like some mystic palace, every home,
A star-walled city, seven-fold fortified.

He at their hest (so Heaven's own book of spheres
Insculpt in arrowy light, ordained) his soul
In the moon's argent streams did imbaptize,
And purified his spirit in the sun;
A handful there of astral fire then seized,
And hid it in his bosom like a flower;
From whence all sacred light was kindled here.

One with all truth, he held himself divine
While e'er he breathed; a flowering branch of light,
That by intense devotion shed a bloom

Of luminous beauty round the blinded mass;
A part supreme of the all-whole supreme;
Perfection in perfection perfected;
Abstracted from the world and gained to God.

Whirled in a wingéd chariot with the skies
Down through the planetary gates of light
And lunar valves descending, earth again
He raught, and, mingling with its chequered race,
On the far fields of fire his God adored.

TIME's arid streamlet through its glassy gorge
Slid ceaseless; and the sphere-experienced now,
Like to the pine, that, from its own sweet fruit,
Springs into crowned perfection, from that crown
Again educing its delicious end,
Fell, with a falling star, into the breast
Of a mild nymph, who by the muse-loved bank
Of sweet Ilissus slumbered. Sore amazed
She watched the growing wonder of her side,
Nor knew the mystery till ten times the moon,
Working like marvellous birth in heaven, and still
As oft recovering crescent purity,
Ushered the throbbing secret into light,
That he his starry ancestry might hail.

Witting right well what 't was to fall from Heaven,
From the immovable star-plane to the prime
Conceptacle of motion, moonwards, through
All spheres in graded order, to the orb
Where dwells, in secret cell, the hermit Life;
His lot he knew, and straightwise calmly went
His heaven-inquiring way, how best he might
Win back the death-lost birthright of the skies.

Plunged in primæval darkness he began,
From the first breathings of the universe,
His godlike quest. By all the elements
He was advised and aided. The vast sea
Absolved him of all soil of sin; the earth
Embraced him as a child in her dark breast,
And of her life the active passion taught;
Fire lent him torches kindled at the shrine
Of some volcano's mighty altar, reared
By mightier nature to the almighty sire,
That he might light the holy to their end.

Air gave him access to the gods, and made
Her boundless reaches, rich with ore of light,
Common to man and all divinities;
The æthereal fields of fire impalpable,

Where the pro-kosmial forms of thought abide,
Divine, of God projected, won his soul,
With pure ingenerate beauty, to explore
Mind's genial mysteries; theirs true life alone.

But though all helped him, none could satisfy:
The course and destiny of that he sought
Was from him hid in Hades. Many a rite
Mysterious, secret, sacred, night and day,
With numbers, with a winnowed few, alone,
Yea sole, at last, he pressed through, till to him
The sun and moon, the glorious twins of light,
God's golden seal, God's silver seal, grew dim
To the self-luminous truth in Hadean halls
Which shining showed the soul, whose fate he urged,
The bride-queen of the God that sought her love,
And dowered her with Elysium's diadem.

Rapt to the breast of fontal Deity
Divine embraces there received he, both
Adoring and adored, by gods themselves
Worshipped and men, he moved felicitous;
The radiant serpent nestling in his breast
And twining round his waist, caducean. Thence
Regenerate, and divergent weal and bale,

Bound to the sovran sceptre still of power,
In the necessitous knot of life and love
Assigning, godlike to the universe,
Consociate of divinity, he viewed,
With starry and all sympathizing eye,
The sublunary realms of deathly life;
Felt the assimilant influences of heaven
Flash through his soul with lightning joy, and meet
Reply in earth-born fulminations made;
Saw the precontinence of the whole by God
Within Himself, and ebb of Being's sea.

Blessed with all visions holy and divine,
Communion holding only with the wise,
Silent in light (the radiant lizard loves
And lives in light, himself all constellate)
With Truth he joyed (as when the moon, disguised
Like naked nymph, her limbs of light revealed
To him, enamored, on the Latmian hill,
Whose touch was inspiration, whose embrace
Deific, seemed absorption into heaven);
Abstinent of all matter, every cause
Of mental perturbation, base desire,
Eradicate and razed, the lunar ark
Of pure regeneration awed he viewed;

Beheld the æternal husbandman of heaven,
Who sowed with star-seed all the wilds of space,
Scattering the worlds broadcast upon his way;
And to that tilth cœlestial set his hand.

But not descent alone knew he; from where
Earth's Atlantean horizon upheaves
The inconceivable convex, to the sum
And polar point of light he passed, and thence,
As at earth's natal movement, downwards struck,
Through starry strophès and conversive glide
Of orbs that round the ever-festive sun,
And unformed stars, to heaven's immortal gates;
And as all nature animate on earth
Began with life amphibious, so fore-starred
By the cœlestial crab, with whom the world
Its eastward march commenced,—(for truly earth
Crept ere she flew upon the breathing winds,
Rounding the void inane,—and gradual all
Accomplish due perfection,)—he between
The aselline starlets and the manger dim
Won, studious of the universal life;
Isis' twin godlings, silence and the light,
Showed him their common immortality;
The bull with horns star-nebbed; the ram, disk-crowned;

And fish Euphratean, taught their varied life,
Their spheral natures and spiritual hopes;
For of all these the denizens aspire
Towards the invisible and paternal heavens;
By his æthereal side he paused who pours
(On templed tablet traced), from ample urn,
The first effusion into chasmy space.
That starry stream and matter prime of worlds,
River of God, on silver wings he swam,
By goat-fish, crocodile, or horned whale,
The mountain-swallowing deluge embleming,
And demigod, who voluntary died,
Aiming star-headed arrow winged with light;
Who taught him there sidereal truth as once
The Larissæan youth Parnassian lore;
By scorpion death-stinged, or Typhonian snake,
He boldly hied; and by the assessor stern,
With rod and balance poised, saw weighed the worlds,
And heard the utmost measurement of time;
Beside the maid fruit-bearing he espied
Her new-born starlet, the god altar-throned,
By all the moons encircled of the year;
And lion, hearted with a royal orb,
Which nigh his shaggy shoulder bore the sun,
Invincible, who, 'neath his yoke of light,

Compels the starry armies of the heavens;
He, thief divine, heaven's starry apples steals,
And glories in the feat; in slumber lulls
Air's orbéd eyes o'erwatchful of the earth;
Unfolds the love of beauty to the gods;
Fills earth with nymphs and heroes, and their seed
Semi-divine; usurps the throne of heaven;
From west to east, foot-swiftest of all things,
Courses the sky; withdraws the moon from earth;
Yet mindful of the time when once with eye
Extinct he groped the concave, till the flock,
Ram-marshalled, 'scaped the darkness of the sun,
And victims, death devote, renewed their life;
And once, by night o'ercome, his locks of light
Shorn,—but Time's temple hath not fallen yet;
Nor yet the Herculean pillars, east and west,
Embracing, hath he hurled to total wreck;
Nor yet the gates of glory gone for aye.

There resting on that regal sphere of light
And happiest altitude, he stood and knew
The æthereal essence of creation; saw
The world of mind roll Godwards through all time,
And the circuitous course of good in life,
Till temporal and æternal coalesce;

For stars are signs of constellated truths
Æternal in the intelligible heavens;
Saw that to every world, wherever placed,
Shine other eagles, serpents, crosses, crowns;
That hydra sins of foul corruption bred
Subdued by grace are glorified; whose yet
Unceasing sibilation sounds, through life,
To arms, the saintly combat of the soul.
Him, therefore, the celestial fiend, who breathes
The breath of death and from his mortal mouth
Empoisons air; beneath whose fatal fangs
Creation sickens and all evil reigns,
He fought, to free from fear the affrighted world;
Until the all holy and regenerant star
Rise that shall rise, and into light transmute
The sacred body of the universe;
And Truth, triumphant virgin and divine,
All virtues heavenly and humane fulfilled,
All suffering, all o'ercoming, up and rule,
Sweet saviour of celestials. She his brow
There sealing with a seven-rayed star, in sign
Of victory achieved, around his neck
Olympian wrapped the mantling skies moon-clasped;
The solar bowl of blended blood and wine,
That sparkles in the prototypic skies,

The chalice handed aye of Nemesis
To lips oracular, dreadless he received,
And life reviving quaffed; whence, clear in sight,
He saw the rise of spirit, in its prime
And purity sublimely ignorant, long,
Till after lapse and forfeiture of bliss,
All earthly suffering, and descent of death,
Dearer to him and lovelier for her fall,
Celestial love the soul immortal wed.

Thence tracing the unseen course, which earth shall
tread,
In a no fabulous future, when the will
Of man, so oft transversive of the truth,
With God's shall coincide, and all be light, —
The bright abyss he soared, but left unnamed;
Whether in lapse of ages it shall trend
Towards the Orphëan light, — of old there held
Type of concordant spheres, — or southern sign,
That in the heavenly roodloft starwise beams,
Stands untranslated in the book of God.
The book of nature He himself hath writ
God still delights to read, and star by star
Unfolds the volume of the universe
Fate-clasped; in time and order by Him fixed.

Thus conversant with gods, immortal, he
The pure perfection whence he fell regained,
Gifts pleni-solar, and præ-astral powers,
Prophetic, and mnemonic of all time,
With added wisdom of all ill and good.
The gates of death he passed and doubly lived,
The gates of life, whereby the blest ascend;
Then drave his dragon chariot round the world,
Lashing with lightnings till they sweated fire.
Gaming with golden dice, he of the Sun
Won thrice his light; of ocean, deep by deep,
His boundless realms; of earth, her countless lands;
But their own bade them take again, while he
One moment merged in that leviathan womb,
And through the starry tabernacles borne,
By seven bright maids immortal, (gleeful they
At the lost brightness refound,) from the depths
Of heaven's sidereal river drew and drank
The lymph divine of light, the dew of life.

Throughout the vast passivity he passed
All active, through the grand ellipse of life,
And circular progress of the wind-winged world,
Safe from all storms of fate and floods of ill,
And dreadless of the gorgon mask of Death.

All nature gladdened in those rites; the sea
Avouched his safety; fire would harm him none;
Danced moon and sun around him with their stars;
And the Great Father solemnly rejoiced.

Hallowed of heaven and consecrate of man,
He in his palm the eye-crowned sceptre swayed,
And belted sate enthroned and diademed.

Time's sand-dry streamlet through its glassy strait
Rilled restless; and the heaven-invested seer,
Of rainbow born and dragon stony-winged,
While lineally descended of the sun,
And cradled in regenerative tomb,
The orbit of his life renewed. Beside
The stream that through the midst the beauteous isle
Disparts, tree hid, tree hight, (where haply once
The tyrant lion of some cavernous land
To lesser brutes his deathful law dispensed,
Or with the jungle monarch, ivory-tusked,
Held thunderous parley by the tidal swamp,)
Or where the wave, prophetic and divine
From Bala pours; or on the far-off coasts
Of sacred isle, where lunar mysteries
Are solemnized, as erst, and consummate;

Or, 'mid rude dwellings, once the abode of gods
Of hostile faiths, he lowly dwelled, and learned
On his cold knee, before white-bearded Eld,
From Truth's pale lips her everlasting lay,
And deepest, pithiest lore. For thrice nine years,
Through fits of silence, loneness, fasting, toil,
He fought the foe of spirit and subdued.
The thrice-thinned juices of the all-healing plant,
With moon-dews mingled and eye-brightening charms
The unseen to see, himself invisible;
Honey, and berries red of the eërie wood,
Oakcorns and apples, roots and wheaten cates,
His fare and bever formed for twice an age,
With amber flowing mead at moonéd feasts.

He on the circular mount of safety dwelled,
Taught by cœlestial serpent of the sun;
And learned his solar syllables of fire,
And the moon's mountain alphabet (first conned
By them of old, who, in the ark-hive, warred
Sole with a world of waters, warred and won);
And from the rock, cave-crested, downwards led,
Eye-bounden, by the hand of priestess maid,
Who in prophetic solitude abode;
Through the returnless valley, and thick-branched

Forest, whose trees sore strived, with audible groans,
Their steps to intercept, they thrid their way
Shorewards, to where the hazy sea of death
Broke in black billows, soundless though their wrath,
Intangible its waters. Pacing thence
Into a skiff of grisly marble, they,
O'er those mysterious straits quick steering, made
The isle of blessed ghosts, with plenar breath
That bright witch-virgin, silent but inspired,
The filmy sail o'erfilling, and called up
With the spirit of her breath so fierce a storm,
That with their madding moil the waves themselves
Inflamed; fire boiled; and all the waters blaze.

Conductress! O enchantress! lead me back,
He cried, among the nations. They, meanwhile
Returning, she to him like power imparts,
Which freely he receives. The o'erflooding stream
Whose freshets grieved the villager, he froze
With one blast of his breath; then, from its bed,
Like to a glistening snake, the evil tore,
And hung it high, stream upwards, on the hill.

Against a foamy torrent in a skiff
Of glass, he fountwards steered, nor, rock-dashed, brake;

Till in the stilly birth-pool, anchored safe
Amid translucent shadows, he, beyond
All watery bruit a stone-cast, rode serene.

By living ladder, to the enchanted chair
Gigantic, hewn of huge and holy rock,
Lifted, he sate and all the stars outstared,
Gazing them down, dog, centaur, eagle, bull;
And the unmeasured monsters of Heaven's main
Came foaming to his feet and licked his hand.
They his heart lighted up; and he from them
Taught wisdom to the serpent; and to spheres
Their secret revolution, silent song,
And sacred circuition of the sun.

Impowered in turn by these with chariest charms,
The sun, from dawn to night-noon, he outeyed
From the peaked mountain which commands the world.
And earth's penumbral pinions, by her side
Quivering; with him he leaped in joy of life
Immortal proven, hand in hand, through air;
In sign whereof, on that most holy day,
Heaven's globéd flower, whose perfume is the light,
Rose from the polar-north perpend, and not
With slow initial motion from the west,

As theretofore, in ages lost to time,
Ere coal-palm leaved, or pristine pine, now tombed
In earth's sepulchral centrals, had put forth
The mystic life-cone, fern her feathery stem.

On many an altar at his beck the sun
Shot down his shafts of light; the heavens and he
Spake miracles together, and exchanged
Sojourn of spirits; for the heavenly came
Earthwards, and heavenwards went the earthlier.

Between the fires of sun and moon he passed
Benefic; and throughout the hallowed land,
As at the great rekindling, when the heavens
Shall shine with souls in galaxies, as now
With stars, beneath the priest creator's hand, —
Dealt forth to all the sun-incepted light.

Upon the pyrameidal mount of law
He sat, and soothed the nations at his feet,
Urging in wavy tribes their yearly right
Of blessing, and prescriptive gift of fire,
The dues of doom, the balance and the chain;
The starry chain which links all souls to God.

Born from between the trinal clifts, age-ripe,
In love and wisdom he all power consummed;
Midst of the luminous circle where the one
The twain o'ertowers, and from the twain the third
Derives, the whole one trine; and where the sun,
Beside his sacred city, as the close
Of the great year comes sæcularly round,
Descends, and sings and dances through the night;
Harping to all around his own high deeds,
The grain and fruit he ripens, and the breasts
Of living things he animates anew,
In countless generations, times untold;
The many-nationed orbs he fills with joy;
The many-citied lands he roofs with light;
The many-islèd seas he sows with life;
While o'er them all his golden robe he casts,
Stands the arch mystic, celebrant of Heaven:
And as the solar song in silence ends,
All gazing on the firmamental eye,
Responsive to the light, his lyre he lifts,
And sings with sphæral power creation past:—

God was, alone in unity. He willed
The infinite creation; and it was.
That the creation might exist, His Son,

And that it might return to Him, the Spirit
Disclosed themselves within Him; thus triune
But as the all-made must of necessity
Inferior be to its creator, thus
Arose the infinite imperfect, time,
The spirit-host angelic, heavenly race,
Brute life and vegetive, electric light,
Matter and fleshly form; to human souls
Nine generations from æternity.
But God, who is Love, decreed it should return
By pure regeneration unto God;
Wherefore was need that He from whom came life
Should taste death, but in tasting swallow up;
That commune with all creatures might be made,
On this hand, and on that, with Deity.
Thus death and evil expiate ends divine;
The Spirit the imperfect hallowing, death
The Son; the soul regenerate hies to God;
And as in radial union with the point
Infinite, both in greatness place and power,
Lives with the maker and the all-made in love.

In anticlinal order next he hailed,
And interpendent harmonies of song,
Gentle and fine as the concurrent curve,

Perpetual, in the orbits of twin stars,
The future fates and times divine to be;
The negative divinity of man;
The holy and unhappy blent in bliss
At last; the passed unburthened of her doom,
Like conscience of her self-secretive truth,
Condemning conduct but assuring life;
And when, in that vast volume penned of God
Whose text is earth, whose margin is the main,
His everlasting service shall become
One hymn triumphant, jubilant; from all
Doubt or fear free, remorse or self-reproach;
Serenely issuing from the soul of man,
As from the lee of the o'ershadowing moon,
Suddenly perfect, glides a star occult.

Ceased he; and all apart as the altar stone
Of some Titanic temple, reared in eld,
The golden and gigantic age of earth,
By sacred groves, sun-founts and seats of gods
Enringed, and radial avenues of rocks
All navelling in the sanctuary divine,
There at the universal mother's shrine,
Round whom nine hallowed maidens minister,
He worships in the granite-winged fane.

From wisdom's pearl-lipped bowl the draught he drains
Of pure oracular rede, which rendereth men
As gods wise, and illumed with day-like light:
Then with his white wand cleaves the skies, and gives
To kings their laws, to states their faith, to both
The empire he disdeigns. To all he makes
Patent his end, (truth's honey-gilded draught
Boding him this,) and on the central shrine,
The great dark stone, symbol of darkness' self
All-emanant, and the divine obscurity
Of Deity, as on the heart of light,
Fanned by the sacred winds, which fail not then
Due service to the high departing soul,
Tempests and clouds the playthings of his power,
Serene in will, and willing not to be,
Upright he sate, and eyed the sun, and died.

Initiate, mystic, perfected, epopt,
Illuminate, adept, transcendent, he
Ivy-like, lived, and died, and again lived,
Resuscitant. On high his nest he wove
In the strange tree whereof man first was made,
Whose roots reach down to hell, whose topmost bough
Waves its bright leaflets in the airs of heaven,
And communed with the universal life,

Beloved of lightning for its kindred birth,
That vivifies its veins; until possessed
Of all that could be known, the whole he knew;
Cropped where they grew the flowers of learning,
massed
In meadowy beds, and bright with fragrant dew.

Carving with glyphic art immortal runes,
That rule the reluctant spirits of the dead,
On living wood, with primal matter oned,
Which breedeth still betimes celestial fruit,
He, arrow-like, launched forth — heaven is a bow
The chord whereof is earth — and charmed his way
Led by prismatic clue through spheres and skies,
Fire, ice, and scalding venom-floods of hell,
To prove all sacred truth within himself;
To test all holy virtues; and to know
The sovereign Master of the universe,
Who hallowing, blessed his hemispheral aim.

To him too came from Preadamic kings
The shield of power, graved with seven mystic seals,
Transcript of stars that signalized release
Jointly, to him, of their domain o'er earth;
Incaved wherein, the book of light he conned

And read inscribed the truths which hallow heaven,
Yea, viewed all mysteries not ineffable
And ne'er to be unsealed, denude themselves
Into two truths, of God and man, they one;
The light enlightened and enlightening light.
From scrolls Sethæan and the columned lore
Of lands unknown, or which was wisely hid
In pre-diluvian volumes, (lost, alas!
Neath those ebullient waters which engulfed
The foulnesses and sins of a naught world;
Or if conserved, in purity conserved
Only, within that temple subterrene,
Gem-pillared and nine-porched, from dust-doomed eye
Secreted, by one deathless reared, ere yet
Translated to the bosom of his God,)
The secret orders of the sphere he learned,
Not yet to be revealed, nor till the end,
The coming incandescence of the globe;
Then let the Heavens astounded, list to Fate.
By divine science and cœlestial art
He for the cause of the dear nations toiled,
And augusted man's heavenly hopes that so,
Child of the vast and universal man,
(Man archetypal, starry and terrene,
Whose head is high above the angelic seven,

Whose heart the sun,) he might, by awful rites
Hinted in sacro-sanctities of the wise,
From knowledge of æternal names acquest,
Illumined intellect and pure desire,
Adhæsion with Divinity achieve.

His eyes, from constant converse with the stars,
Conceived an astral virtue, and his brow,
Cooled with their fragrant breath, grew bright; his soul,
One and compatient with the life of time,
Rose kosmical with all God's great designs;
And so on earth their luminous life enjoyed,
The unapparent and essential fates.
For God, when first He form'd man, so insphered,
And veiled with beauty all compulsive power
(Necessity, when isolate becoming
By limited mutations of the will,
A self-determinate freedom and minute)
In the individual soul, that none but they
Who extasie divine enjoy, agnize
The universal impulse, but so act
As though they ordered all things of themselves,
And heaven were but the registrar of earth.
In nations, creeds, and ages, men can trace,

Star-writ in night's imperial book of fate,
The world's vast destinies; but void, alas!
Of introvertive vision, not their own.

To God soul-bounden, as some sacred orb,
Content in its own brightness to outshine,
Or be outshined by others, he the whole
Perceived to him pertain, and him to all;
And found, by nature's ominous sympathies,
His private fates proceed, like-paced, with God's,
And their fore-fixèd purposes concur.

In temple-like totality he held
His heart, hypæthral, open to all heaven;
And to all earth her future and her passed,
Magician-like, divulges from his charts.

As when of old some king of men might trail
Between two hosts his glittering spear, and mark
War's red meridian, in that dusty score
Graving the death of empires and the birth
Of new thrones, till in flow of years arise
One who erases from the face of earth
That sanguine wrinklet, so the universe
Contentiously divaricate, he shows

Made one in spirit with eternity;
For man divine shall reign; shall cede to God
All rights, all laws, both priestly and externe,
Vulgar and regal. One conclusive claim
All passed confirms, and hallows all to come.

To every mind the meaning it hath meant,
Though blindly blundering on through clouds of speech,
And crowds of forms, in surface differing,
He, sole interpreter, with holy rod
Hermetic, explicates, and proves for peace;
That all divisive theories but denote
A secondary standing of the soul,
And partial knowledge only of the truth;
Whose faith is truest into all projects
That blessed secret, unitive and divine,
The totalizing wisdom of all creeds,
The faith æternal and entire, which us
Ones with the heavens; and that in all worlds, though,
By the imperfect mean it passeth through,
(As told in mysteries tauro-serpentine,)
Good begets evil, evil brings forth good
In blest regeneration; and that God,
Who all creates, all saves, all sanctifies;
Man, in himself, both sacred and profane.

These are the laws of light, sweetly severe,
Which show that what disorder seems, gives proof
Of order loftier than the mind of man
(Who holds, because his little eyeball 's round,
The infinites must be all orbicular)
Pews in its petty systems: and these laws
He, sagest Theocrat, whose church is heaven,
Whose state all earth, whose law the book of God,
The sole converter of the universe,
Kept in his heart with holy fire; and thus,
In changeful perfectness, the wheel of life
Trolled underneath his feet, till he beheld
Grim, o'er the funeral hatchment of the world,
Death's empty helm yawn; and his toil was done.

Like Mekkah's milky stone, which wastes away
Beneath the kiss of worshippers, so life
Darkens and wanes beneath its crowd of cares;
While Time's last sands silt up the streams of soul,
Less, gradually decreasing, less and less.

As when in northern marches dies a man
Well famed of men, for virtues, or for birth,
Great grows the press of mourners round his grave,
In ceremonious silence; great the show

Of lawny weepers lifted to dim eyes,
As slowly slideth the bier downwards; all
Bare-headed, wordless; so with simplest pomp
Of their mere presence, all earth's kindred creeds
(And his was perfect, he believed in God,
In God the Spirit, and God-man, the Son)
Clung round his heart and sanctified his end.

All gifts were therefore given him, seals and signs
Of radiant force and triply perfect power.
The spirit of earth to him his double key,
Defensive from all ills, all goblins, gave;
Wisdom her adamantine seal, and Truth
Her sapphire signet; Love his ruby ring.
Spirits and apparitions of pure grace
Came shadowy round at his interior will;
And one in chief, of angel charm, would come,
(As though within her breast a dawn divine,
Insensibly were orbing into life,)
Perfused with roseate radiance, like a star
Veiled in creative fire-mist, who his eye
With spiritual clear-sight filling, showed
Truths past all search, all height, all depth, all bound,
Of interspheral orders, and their rise,
Action, and central end. She in her own

Bright virtue him embracing gave his soul
In secret, sweet assumption into heaven;
And both with filial and parental bliss
Imbued, bade wander through the golden plains
With diamond blooms bestarred; but ere she left,
Lest he celestial pleasures might profane,
Commingling speech thereof with mundane things,
By the thrice sacred kiss of secrecy,
An adamantine oath, his lips she sealed.

The mount of shadow earth each night uprears,
The sun each morn planes down, he clomb, and held
Parley with orb and angel as they passed
Self-luminous on their quests; his nebulous thoughts
Grouping in firmamental unities.
At his will-fraught and evocative word,
The strange star brightened largelier, and poured forth
Its voice of light, or speechlessly withdrew
Into its azure chambers, which the wide
Abyss, precipitous, of space, o'erhang.

The spirit-world, thus lovably coerced,
Did homage, in such service deeming them
Triumphant; and reciprocal with all,
All loyally he ruled. Thereat rejoiced,

All wisdom in one whisper they conveyed,
All language uttered in one mystic word
Wrought of sun-heated fire-flame, first pronounced
Among the angels proximate to the throne;
Where cloaked with threefold light the all Divine,
The infinite point, the circumfused Supreme
Deific dwells, whose thoughts are tinged with heaven,
His own æternal and impropriate bliss,
As clouds and mountains with the noonday light.

For, even as darkness, self-impregned, brings forth
Creative light, and silence, speech; so beams,
Known through all ages, hope and help of man,
One God omnific, sole, original,
Wise wonder-working wielder of the whole
Infinite, inconceivable, immense,
The midst without beginning, and the first
From the beginning, and of all Being last.

A SPIRITUAL LEGEND.

A SPIRITUAL LEGEND.

THERE were who spiritual legends feigned,
Half lofty, half profound, not nigh half true,
Believed, or seemed; whereof one instance hear,
As erst by early Gnostic of the Nile
Taught; garnished and enlarged in later years.

Ere all, in ancientry æterne, was God
(Holy and blessed alway be His name)
In essence inconceivable. He in space
As luminous fulness, pure perfection dwelled,
And in an infinite unity.
Coæterne
With God (for ever blest and worshipped be
His name) and contrary to Him as good
Was matter, mother of all evil, end
And centre, caused by Deity nowise.

Light
And darkness are the emblems of these powers,
And ensigns. From their opposition comes
Of good and evil like necessity;
While death and body, life and soul, compugn.

From the All Being Father (Love his name,
Mercy and Grace) the Spirit first was born,
The spirit, thence the Reason, called the Word;
From reason, Providence; from providence
Came Power and Wisdom; wisdom Righteousness
Joyful brought forth, and power almighty, Peace.

God's light through His trine essence self-reflected,
As through an infinite prism, and like the sun,
Of heaven's great bow the sevenfold hues producing
These seven blessed spirits, attributes divine
Which do His essence designate, evolved.
He, in His own substantial deity,
The same, to whom the septenary stars
And days of time be consecrate, conceived,
Issued and vivified, with Him to live;
Æonian beings of divinest strain.

Of these the twain, hight Power and Wisdom, joined

In holy union, forthright generate
Angels of highest rank and noblest force,
In nature godlike, and in number such
As saintly calculations dedicate
To heavenly orders; such, on Thracian mount,
The maiden muses, sacred to the sun,
Who, hand in hand, with ominous laurel crowned,
Roses or stars, do hymn the universe.

Pure and beneficent these; inferior still
To their progenitors, as they to those
From whom they boast their birth. These first composed
A heaven wherein companionably to dwell,
And to delight each other. From them sprang,
Native to thrones and glories unconceived,
Angelic generations, rank on rank,
And heaven on heaven, innumerably spread
Down through the starry crystalline, in clouds;
Each order forming its own cœlestial home;
Like numbered with the daily circlets of the year.

These all the dominance supreme confessed
Of the Æternal, in one mystic word
Abraxas, since, on many a jasper gem,

Of talismanic and regenerant force,
Insculptured, — hailing Him their total lord
And Spirit Father.
They, meanwhile, who dwelled
Of the angelic nations, in the last
And lowest round of all the heavens which stretched
Its confines to the dark material mass,
Malignant, uncreate, inert, self-lived,
Which lay, a weltering chaos, deep below,
Felt, as their glittering pinions oft they poised
In level flight above its stormy face,
And gulfs of unpierced wonders, vast desire,
Heightened by warm debate among themselves,
Their neighboring state to soothe and purify;
And form, leave sought of God, first, and obtained,
Since theirs the limits of the angel realm,
A race of beings fitted therein to abide,
Branch forth and govern other lower lives,
To be for their behoof created.
Fired
With this imperial and divine intent,
Through the three hundred three score spheres and five
Of super-imminent hierarchies, flew up
A band eclect of the æthereal powers,

Who carried rapture on their snowy wings,
Unto the footstool of the omnipotent One.

There, breathing low their wishes and desires,
Made holy by the end, to enlarge God's reign
And purify and dignify the mass
Of matter, dark and void, with creatures apt
For such estate, though lower far than they,
God hearkened, granted leave to do their will,
And proffered more even then.
Plenipotent
The suppliant assemblage returned; their brows,
As through circumvolant myriads on they passed,
Bright with the sense of God's imputed power,
Flashing delight. Benevolent they went,
Creative they returned; and to their hosts
Of fellow-immortals all their triumphs tell.

Grand was the joy throughout those radiant tribes,
Lift to the zenith of celestial bliss,
And instant impulse urging to begin
The work orbific; glorying in their plans
Of future suzerainty and wide-spread sway
Among new worlds of creatures yet to be.

God taking thought, Himself, of sun and star,
With whom to think, indeed, is to create,
Those heavenly isles of light, of light profound,
Light within light, the bright abodes of bliss; —
Chaos, the rude conglomerate, co-æterne
With all Divinity, they first commenced
To soften, free and sever by degrees,
From multiform confusion, into fixed
And elemental sections.
                                        Thence appeared
The all genetic waters and clear depths
Of air's unseen but palpable flood, wherein
The water-mountains melt, in themselves drowned;
The youthful breeze; and fierce gigantic storms,
Allies of evil and confœderate fiends,
Which the sun's variable heat obey;
The virgin fire, inviolably pure;
And earth's all mothering bosom.
                                                Soon, distinct,
Ocean and continent, sea, desert, plain
Mineral and vegetive, concrete, complete,
By separate hand, each Power a separate type
Framing, to grace his will, or prove his force,
Of stone, earth, tree, plant, shrub, grass, herb, or flower,
Mountain, or isle, or river, lake, or well.

The angels made the solid earth; its rocks
Chaotic and amorphous, petrified fire,
Granitic, oolitic; sand and lime;
Igneous and aquatic beds of stone
Upheaving or collapsing, seemed, in turn,
The awful sport of some Titanian arm,
Whose elbow, jogged by earthquakes, wryed the pole.

The angels wrought the mountains, bulk by bulk,
And chain by chain, serrated or escarped,
Or coal-red burning from Vulcanian forge;
Hekla and Mouna Roa and Auvergne;
Tuxtla; and Tongarari, southwards isled;
By savages beset, who deem, when dead,
Their chieftain's eyes translated into stars;
Andes and Himalaya's heavenly heights;
Dhawalaghiri's pinnacle supreme,
And Chuquibamba's cone of roseate snow;
The hill Altäic named the almighty god,
By Tchudic tribelets of the age of mounds;
Higher than lark can soar, or falcon fly,
Cloudlet, or visible vapor scud, it stands;
Oural, and Balkan; Alp, and Alp pennine;
The magnet mountain which directeth earth,
Brainlike, ensconced beneath her snowy crown;

Lupata's mighty spine; Lamalmon's pass,
O'ertoppling; Abba Yaret's glittering peak;
Ankobar's, Medra's ranges; all that ring
The desert heart of slave-land, or thence stretch
To the Cape of Storms, and lion of the sea;
And Erebus antarctic, fenced with ice.
Marmoreal mountains, by their radiant hand
Polished to white perfection, so to prove
A beauty beyond use, the angels piled;
Kailasa, and the æthereal mount Meru,
Dazzling the sun with gems; Larnassus green;
And Athos, and Montserrat, holy heights,
Mountains of monks, and hills of eremites;
And that Kropakhian, wonder-mountain named,
Without, within; whose central fount obeys,
With an obsequious volume, the moon's wane
Or increment; and that funereal spur
Of dark black marble that beglooms the air;
Or, walling earth, the spirit-haunted Kâf,
With many a mythic marvel crowned of eld;
That crystal mount (cloud crested, once it stood
In western Tucuman) with bright reply
Answering the solar messages of light
As equal equal; deep below its base,
O'erarched a navigable river runs,

Rumbling its rock-pent breakers, white with wrath;
Or where, 'mid central isthmus (on each hand
Pacific and Atlantic tides) is built
Coy Iximaya and the precipitous gates
Of that recondite capital, haply doomed
To vanish into cloudland; the idol rock
Mackinaw vaunts, where red braves, worshipping,
Prophetic murmurs of oracular shell,
Shrined in its ark, hearkened; and holy Tor
In many a land to deity devote;
Divine Alborz, the holy mountain named,
Where, sunlike, the Simorgh, all-wise, abode,
Moon-peaked; or mount oracular of the gods,
Olympus blest; and either sacred Ide;
In that bright isle where Rama reigned, the peak
Whereon the print of Bouddha's foot (esteemed
The last of gods) or Adam's, first of men,
Hallows the land to pilgrims of all creeds;
And thee, dread Sakhrat, pendent once in air,
Now fixed; once soft as heart of man to grasp
Prophetic; 'neath whose saturated roots
All fountains rise; plomb underneath the new
City of God; upon whose crest shall stand
The stern archangel when with judgment trump
He hails the generations of our race,

Those living, those whom hollow Hades holds:
All these and countless more the angels wrought,
While dear they were to God and kind to earth.

The angels trenched the rivers; and unsealed
The secret wealth of many a fountainous hill;
Where Oby, now, or sunny Kour, for wine,
And virgin gold, and hapless virgin slaves,
Renowned, flows; holy Boug; or warlike Don;
Or Po, by Goths imprayed with murderous rites;
Or that, beneath whose bed the wasteful Hun,
God's scourge, lies coffined; (so shall onetime sleep
All evil, 'neath the covering flood of love;)
Where Darro, by the mountain of the sun,
Sweeps with steep wave; or Guadiana dives;
Or where the rivers flow, of life, of death;
Volga, or legendary Rhine; or Rhone,
Vine-banked; or Thames, with the world's wealth and
 that
City of cities, crowned with golden spires,
The towers of God, enriched; Isis, or Cam,
For love of wisdom famed, and Clutha, sung
By warrior harps of old days; there, where now
Ohio broadens, or gross Missouri dims
The deepening sire of floods, aye tiding on

His current deluge to the gulfy breast
Of central seas; or, Niagara hurls,
Precipitant, his thunderous waters down
Their crescent steep; or silver river, south,
Through grass-flowered Pampas pours recoiling wave,
Prescient of blood fraternal ere the end;
His face with intertwining snakes alive,
Thick as the savage tribes that tread around;
From Boreal ice-floes where all waters cease,
To Magellanic straits and land of fire;
Where pagan Saghalien, iced to his bed
Three seasons yearly, steals; or sacred Sinde;
Or Chandra-bagha, holy to the moon;
Or Brahmapootra, fling o'er bordering meads
Their annual floodlets fruitful; or Hoang-ho
Through fragrant tea-fields winds; or where, with palms
Embanked, barbarian Quorra; there men trade
In ivory, gold, and blood; nor far remote,
Who the divine child, babe æterne, adore,
Unconscious deity; or Zenhagal,
With gum-woods girt; or Gambia; or, rock-brinked,
That by Mataman, townless land, rolls; that
Kaffrarian, endless called; and (only found
Late-while) who through the island continent glides,

His current dwindling seawards, dark Moray;
While Araluen's golden-footed nymph,
From rocky urn cœrulean, teems her tide;
Hydaspes; branchy Gyndes, fabulous floods;
Orontes, on whose slopes the wine of gold
In ripening globules glows, whereof, at eve,
Roused from his stony solitude of walls
By turbaned traveller with his camel train,
Not seldom sips the hospitable monk,
His cup commending to the bearded lip
Of smiling stranger, garrulous in signs;
And that sabbatic river, which to flow
The seventh day ceaseth piously; these all
And more, innumerable, brooklet, beck,
Rill, runnel, rivulet, the angels made,
Administrative of terrestrial wealth,
And will cœlestial, while at one with God;
And rivers subterrene booming through caves
Down to earth's focal fires, still inextinct,
And flaming floods, whence, dashed, they reascend,
Volcanic vapors, and explode the hills;
And linn, and force, and torrent; Corra's foam;
Thy falls, unfailing Rhaiadwr; and thine,
Shoshonee, wreathed with shifting rainbow mists;
And those of Dekkan Ghauts, earth's loftiest leap.

The angels reared the islands; that of yore
Neptunian, where the sea-god righteous ruled,
And his ten sons, now sunken in mid-sea;
And that Panchaian, where Triphylian Jove
Judged from his mountain chair the sacred soil;
The starry islet wandering with the wind,
Pure of all death, the birthplace of twin gods;
For sun and moon præsolar light precedes;
Bacchic and Cytherean isles; those spread
Sporadic or cycladic; Cyprian soil;
And Rhodian, sovereign of the sacred sea;
That isle, the sun's, whose sacred slaughtered kine
(When the bull led the constellated round
Ere by the star of storms, gigantic, smote)
Caused to the wise world-wanderer floods of woe;
The wingèd island, flying round the world,
Walled high with gold-bright crystal, giant-kinged;
And fairy Avalon, still where Arthur rules,
Sole as the sun in heaven his shining shrine;
Stern Hertha's, stained with the sacred blood of man;
Elysian islands, all-felicitous, holy,
Where dwell the blessed Immortals, years divine,
The elemental sequences of suns,
And ages everlasting of the heavens;
And Bolotoo, the paradise of gods,

Far off in western space, a land of shades;
Where, to chance wanderer, for the future bound,
And searching for some secret lost to earth,
Tree, temple, tower, and grove-clad hills present
But permeable forms; through all he stalks,
As through a builded vision; wall and bark,
And cliff, close round the path he passeth through
Unharmed, as water round a diving gull;
Islands of honey, pearls, and gems, and fire;
The isle auriferous, whose minutest rill
Outbids Pactolus; those which clustering pour
Spices, perfumes, oils, incense, and sweet gums,
For human delectation or divine;
Feejee and Papua, men-devouring isles;
Black Hayti, the imperial negro's throne;
Niphon, where, temple-shrined, the golden bull
Butts, first, with fiery horn, the egg mundane;
And that Ogygian, westward, where the sun
Utters his final smile, and gleams his last
Through groves of worship dedicate to Fate;
And those white isles whose pre-antiquity
Transcends all date, the primal seats of gods,
Truth, science, song, and all commanding mind:
All these, and countless more, the angels made,
While dear they were to God and kind to earth.

The angels scooped the lesser seas and lakes;
Baltic, and Midland, soundless; and that womb
Of nations, on whose life-devouring shore,
Far jutting into the black and boisterous deep,
Sebastopolis, key of empire, stands;
The pool Mæotic, worshipped as a god
By Scythic hordes, and Amazonian dames,
Militant, jealous of the dexter breast;
And Caspian, deep below whose silvery wave
God's Eden hideth, and the hallowed glebe;
Aral, Vân, Baikal, holy lake, most vast
Of mountain meres; and Tahtar Kokonor;
Ladoga shoal, deep Leman; isleted
Lomond, subterraneous of access;
And many an iceless and unfathomed pool
On mountain crest, or cowering at the foot;
Ontario, Winnebago, and the Slave;
Yutah's; hard by where the polygamous sect
(Misled by one self-unctioned, not anoint,
Nor golden oil of genius had, nor truth,
Who from the brook the lines of lacquered lead,
Sham angel-forged, dug out; who, after, fell
Shotted with three times Cæsar's trickling wounds,—
Ill-doer he, ill done by) bide their hour,
Dreadless; the great Saline; and Aztek, bowered

With floating pleasaunces, where sailed the swans
Of sway symbolic; Amucu, golden-banked;
Or Titicaca, from whose sacred shores,
Long ages lapsed, the scions of the sun,
Manco Capac and Mama Oëllo, stepped,
Ancestral, to the sceptre of Berou;
Nyassi; Ngami; Mrima; Zana, and that
Lake of the gods, whence Nile, or white or blue;
And wide Nigritian Tschad, still inexplored:
All these, and countless more, the angels made,
While kind they were to earth, and dear to God.

Desert and steppe they smoothed; the waterless sea
(But haply once where tide tempestuous rolled)
Of Aphric Zahara, where the sand-wave heaves
'Neath the simoom, parched, poisoning man and beast;
Kerman's sands salt-white, swept by flamy wind,
Plague-breath'd, which, rousing up the desert dust,
Blinds man's bright eye, and mummifies the frame;
There oft, in arid dell, the cool Suhrab,
Calm mockery of sweet waters, overhung
With green and succulent shrubs — you seem to hear
The ripple of the waves — delusive lurks;
Chamo and Kobi, and the central wastes
Of Austral isle, where range the tameless tribes

Who hurl the bomerang, and, hunger spent,
Do mess on their own blood, disseized of sense;
And those by Baku, where, through wimbled cane,
The holy flame of universal fire
Jets from earth's heart, upwards, to join the sun;
Saronian downs, and many a misty moor,
Where aches the eye with objectless survey,
And long dun moss, they spread prospective; now
With cromlech crowned, gray cairn, or fairy knoll;
Or lithic dance of giants 'neath the moon;
Hurlers or wrestlers who have justly earned
Their stony transformation; or some crew,
Godless, that to the air of fiendly flute
Footed, contemptuous of sabbatic chimes;
Now, days of rest millennial, in their ears,
And voluntary thunders, drone in vain;
And wold and wilderness, where nightly flit
The grosser sprites that haunt these nether skies;
Unmarked, in day's broad glare, the moon's moist eye
Reveals, to those who see, the filmy form;
Drowned lands and verdurous meadows submarine
Where water turtles pasture, wandering free.

Plains planned the Angels then, and champaigns vast,
Savannahs, Pampas, prairies; deeming earth

One garden fit for gods; and seeded them
With grass and herb of every wholesome growth;
Shamrock and trefoil, symbolizing Him,
In lowliest form, who them, their makers, made;
And pulse, and sesamum, and flax, and vetch;
With pearly rice, white wheat, and oats (of old
Gold-washed for the imperial Roman's steed);
Majestic maize, and metamorphic rye;
Millet and lentil, and a thousand grains,
As many and as immixed as Psyche slipped
Through her sad fingers, thrall and lost to Love.

With homeliest roots of thyme and mint and balm
The breezes they perfumed and purified;
And that heart-soothing herb, not less renowned
Than lote, nepenthes, moly, or tolu,
Held to untaint from sin the savage soul;
Weed of the west, that on Virginian plains,
Or fields of fair Habana, moon-beloved,
Lifteth its long lush leaflets; youth and maid
(Scion perchance of some Soudanian chief
By hordes of woman-warriors, slain or slaved),
Tending with nicest tact, till it become,
Beneath the toned and educative hand,
A roll of natural incense; weed, that wild,

Climbs prophet Lebanon; and, fragrant, fumed
Through ambered jasmine, wiles the sultry hours,
By plashing fountain's creamy marbled marge:
(To him who sang man's fall, the eve of life
This lightened; and his restiff heart assuaged,
The pilgrim bard, whose days these closely heel
Of ours, who in the aftermath of time
Live; for fame's harvest long ago was got;)
Vervain and magic haschisch, which endows
Thought with ubiety, and waking mind
Clothes with the dread delight of dreams; and kiff,
Soul gifting with expansive extasie;
Madder and plants stellate, and watchet weed,
By rudest fathers used of the mountain isles,
Three-peaked, the golden, beautiful, and white,
Conclusive of the wisdom of the west;
Orris and henna, for perfume or dye;
Mandrake and onion (hallowed wisely once,
In nome Bubastean, sacred to the moon),
Whose coats concentric figured forth the spheres;
As though considerate nature, who, betimes,
Man's facial features casually reveals
In stony fracture or tree-trunk, reframed
In miniature, that man might ne'er forget,
The holy image of the sphere-filled air,

And earth, embraced by heaven, the core of space.

They with fair fruit-trees earth an orchard made;
With rosy apple, purple fig, sweet pear,
Date, honey-pulped, green glowing olive; peach,
Orange, and citron, with their gilded rind;
Sun-juiced muscat, and all the hallowed vines;
Guava and nectarine, mango, plantain, plum;
And that translucent pome, whose cloudy core,
Seed-studded, glows detected, as it hangs
On its slim branchlet, vibrant in the breeze;
The tree transformed of some unhappy god
(Tale immemorial told in Tonga's isle),
Whose fruit is vital bread, man's noblest food;
And that, lactifluous, from whose flower-tipped stem,
High towering, the Caraccan Indian drains,
At day-dawn, creamy draughts, to all his kin
Dispensing, patriarchal, bowl on bowl;
The vast Baobab, like-aged with ocean's tides,
Within whose cavernous and sepulchral trunk
Meet village senates, lawing peace and war
To dusky tribes, or, in its templed bole,
The idol gods adoring of the land,
Arboreal fane; fair thorn, as yet unkinged,
Unsanctified by woes of brow divine,

(We gild the thorns we put upon Him now,
But, ah! they pierce,) whose berries, blood-like red,
Still speak of holiest, still of heavenly ends:
While dear they were to God and to earth kind,
All these, and countless more, the angels made;
More than infallible engine, for an age,
Accomptant pauselessly, or clerk, on slate
Or abacus ten-stringed, could sum.
With woods
And treeful tracts the provident angels clad
What else were lifeless deserts; where now stretch
Forest and upland frith, and the wide weald
Hercynian, where the demon shadow stalks;
And the Anderidan boscage, by divine
Andate, all-victorious goddess, held;
And glades, where, rambling, in long after years,
The outlawed archer led his banded bows;
Siberian forestage of spiry pine;
Oaks, which oracular in Dodona spake;
And equatorial groves that mat the shores
Of Maracaybo, to Maragnon's streams,
And falls of Tequendama; (these were rent
Ere yet the moon rode aëry;) the hoar woods
Of growth eternal, continental reach,
That all enclose, from gold-rocked Labrador,

To florid lands that seas Columbian lave;
From ocean's gilded sands, by Kalamath,
To silvery Zazaticas and Secklong;
Banyan, and temple cedar; gopher, planned
Ark-wise of God to float man o'er the flood;
Laden with life, hope of the world to be;
With treasures vaster than that bark, whose freight,
(Spoils of the sack of Rome — tyrannic queen,
Of bonded nations ravished — the gilded roof
Of Jove's high capitol, the seven-starred lamp
And golden table of God's temple, won
By Vandal, king self-crowned of earth and sea
And their affiliate isles,) storm-sunk, but served
With ivory thrones and busts marmoreal, gems,
And jewelled caskets, armlets, torques, and rings
And carquanets impearled, and coffered coin
Of conquered states, to startle or adorn
Sicilian sea-nymphs in their billowy play;
Cypress, the leafy mourning nature wears,
Dear to the dead and to the field of God,
Where lurks, in spade-turned furrow, seed death-sown,
Divine seed, to be harvested in heaven;
The poplar native to the land of shades;
Myrtle and ebony; dragon-blooded tree,
Coæval with the stars; sun-hallowed palm;

Sweet-scented sandal, spared for sacred rites;
Walnut and chestnut, beech, and ash, and elm;
Wych-hazel, for divining treasures used;
And ruddy rowan, proof 'gainst blackest spell,
And ghastly charms of witches, air-elate;
And that which, like the skies, tree sad by day,
Buds forth at eve its starry blossoms, bright
And odorous, but in sunlight bloomless mourns;
And that beneficent stem, in islands grown
Named Fortunate of old, whose top, with clouds
Nightly encompassed, soon as morning beams,
From leaf and ramage sheddeth cool bright showers,
Freshening the fountless soil; matron and maid,
God thanking for his daily gift with joy,
Brim high their globular gourds from every bough;
And that once common to the world, but since
To one main isle confined, wayfarer's tree,
Within whose veins condensed the essential dew
Flows fontal; while its flowerets, purely white,
Lamplike, allure the wanderer to the wood,
Where he may shade his limbs, and his lips lave;
That tree all fruitful, first and best of things,
(Such by Damaras deemed; naked and black
Their bodies like to their benighted minds,)
From whose umbrageous branchery human fruit,

Fruit holy, fruit immortal, fruit divine,
In sacred ripeness dropped; or that, mayhap,
Whence, chipped by giant woodman, man, brute, bird,
Fell, flew, or, merged in water, swam as fish;
So fable Arctic folk, tribes sparse and spare,
Whose crooked crones, in glittering huts of ice,
(When the vivific sun, world conqueror he,
Closing in peace his serpentine career,
Quenches in snow his thunder,) to their youth,
Sharpening the bone-tipped javelin for the morse,
Quaint legends gabble of their primal eld.

With arborescent canes and ferns they decked
Marish and mead: and sands and hills, else bare,
With shrubs gum-pithed, gum oozing; such were myrrh,
Camphire, and cassia, spikenard, balsam, clove;
(Angels and all good spirits love perfumes;)
With many an odorous plant, both hill and vale;
Angelica, and honeyed melilot;
Day's-eye and king-cup; fairy foxglove, fern;
And violet, crown of the sad Lesbian muse;
Crocus, pale purple or golden; hyacinth,
Skirting with azure haze the foot of woods;
Asphodel and narcissus, Hadean blooms;
And gore-dyed poppy, dedicate to death;

Moonwort; sweet meadow queen; and silver-weed;
Tulipa, dahlia, sunflower, aster, rose,
Damask and white, of holiest silence sign,
Of love divine, love perfect, love æterne;
The fragrant tuberose scintillating light;
Dianthus, flower of God; and, loved of woods,
The wind-flower, blooming faithful to one day,
As Damon to his friend; the iris, eye
Of heaven; eyebright; and winter's flowers of gold;
The lotus, emblem of the sacred birth
Of all from water, pure as spirit seed,
Snow-blanched, or blue; dew of the sea; and those,
The mistress, and the glory of the night;
The flame-flower, glowing like to carbuncle;
Kamschatka's scarlet lily, foodful root;
Nile born papyr, and serpent-creeping flower;
Sumatra's floral miracle, the font
And baptistry of flowers; the tea-rose pale,
In central flowery realm of brightness born;
Magnolia; and tall Yucca's bell-crowned mast;
Bogota's regal lily, whose broad and raftered leaves
In some calm creek expatiate, wood enzoned;
And that night-blooming marvel which, when all
Its flowery kindred, dew-drowned, sleep, spreads forth
Its radiant cup, and like a midnight sun

Illumes the green gloom, and perfumes the dark:
The watery knot-glass, with the blood divine
Sprinkled, that grew beneath Christ's hallowed rood;
Innumerous, the bright blooms whose fragrant speech
Befitting comeliest love, the orient brides
Wreathe into poësies, the angels wrought,
While dear to God (ere eyes divine yet shed
Immortal tears, as the amber droplets wept
By daughters of the sun) and kind to earth.

The angels then with founts the park mundane
(From Athabascan cape, mornwards, to where
Miako's gilded god, colossal, sits;
From Anadyrsk to Patagonian point)
Graced; cool and tepid; these perennial, those
But intermittent; founts that torches fire;
Founts, that, presageful of the tempest, howl;
That ebb and flow contrarious to the main;
Or synchronous; deep springs of bubbling brine
Inland; sweet waters 'neath the sea; and that
Far scalding, still self-petrifactive fount,
Whose separate wavelets hardening, stone by stone,
Yield mansions to the builders on its banks;
Founts scorching, founts petrific, founts of flame,
Ice-cold to touch; founts honey sweet; the rill

Which, sanguine, staineth gules the bordering flowers;
Fountains of ageless youth and maidenhood;
Fountains of love and of disdain; and that
Which Kai Khosrou, forewarned in sleep, beheld,
(Oracular vision,) and, far journeying, found
At last, but, therein bathing, disappeared;
The burning springs that o'er the Caspian's face
Fear-shrunk, afar their fiery furrows drive;
The serpent source that hisses as it flows,
Whose venemous wave all life instinctive shuns,
One breed alone, connatural, thence exempt;
All these and countless more the heavenly tribes,
Whose names are noted in cœlestial tongues,
Bade forth by the divining wand of will;
All wells on earth, save thine, divine Zemzem,
Through starry strata strained, and musky loam
Of paradise; (there moon-browed maids of light,
Immortal, dwell, and from the lakes of bliss
Their star-cups fill;) — thou afterwards wast born.

Unfathomable caves and moss-green grots,
For mysteries or retreat, the angels made;
For vision and prevision; travelled trance
Of spirit, through cœlestial circles borne
Prophetic; those of Patmos, Paros' isles;

Abdera; or the Arab's desert cell;
The cave Iberian, where Tubal abode,
Which great Alcides, after, amplified;
For magic rites and secrets darkly famed,
Phantoms, and necromantic wonders; wealth
Untold, unhallowed; death to all who sought;
The vaults Tartarian where the Titans groaned;
And those where still the rebel angels hang,
Heel skywards, in hell's antechambers, chained;
Nyont's Æolian arch whence gush the winds
Incessant, sighs chaotic; and those caves,
High pitched, in Erin's isle, or Anglian peak,
With floors prismatic, purple crystalled walls,
O'er-roofed with sparkling spires and pendent stars.

Metal and mineral then the angels wrought,
Gold, silver, copper, iron, and all ores;
Marbles; and gems, of virtues potent signs;
The crystal, prevalent over gods, and hid
Close in the hand, assuring heavenly help;
The achate, wealth abductive, and the mind
Of the immortals gladdening, maiden's love
Winning, man's friendship; jasper, to the gods
Delightsome, and potential bliss to earn;
The topaz, aidant in all holy rites,

Prayer favoring; opal, dear to deities,
Prophetic and heroic; magnet chaste,
Of all-persuasive effluence, speechless power;
The crimsoned coral, emblem of the soul,
Reared in life's stormy deeps, the deeps of death,
From mischief fending and hate's fatal glance;
Sunstone, which every phantom foul dispels;
Oracular starstone, warning weal or ill;
And bloodstone, symbolling earth, the gates of God's
Æternal temple, with the life divine
Sprinkled, prognostic dread; the diamond, sweet
And grateful to the gracious spirit throng;
The starry sapphire of celestial blue;
Ruby and emerald, jacynth, amethyst;
The amber, emblem of divinity,
Which with electric influence soul allures;
The pearl conceived of dew and lightning, type
Of that pure maid-birth yet to bless the world:
Yea, cups of pearl, one pure and solid pearl,
Greater than that in Haleb's slab ingrained,
With natural nimbus (so pre-figuring
The glory round earth's kingliest blood) enringed,
Divinest relic in time's temple niched;
And that smaragdine mirror (their chief toy
Which all the angels wrought, each gifting it

With some unique perfection) after owned
By Israel's wisest, who the tongues of bird,
Brute, angel, men, knew; the king looked therein,
And eyed the passed, of any wished-for age,
Apparent as in life; event, or fact;
And when solicitous of the future, he,
Steering by somewhat steadier than the stars,
Had breathed thereon, with the evanishing reek
From off its disk, he all the coming conned
Limned in that talismanic tablet clear.
Gems larger, lovelier these than all now known;
Richer than those twin rubies, called Cancques,
By kings of Auphir, kings of heaven and earth
Self-titled, oft in angry blood-bath dyed;
Or those that on the seven great gods illume
The hall of gold in royal Arakhain;
Whose heads with diamonds, breasts with rubies flame,
With sapphires, emeralds, pearls, their limbs and feet,
And regal robes, rigid with woven gold;
Brighter than those the eastern soldan's throne
Pavonian star; victorious Britain's now;
Than those bright armlets, adamantine pair,
The sea of light, and mountain, (now from sea
Far severed,) seals and signs sublime of power
O'er west and east; more tempting to the touch

Than all encrusting false Fenella's fruit,
With deadly art contrived; or those by Rhine,
Shrined round the heads embalmed of sainted kings;
Finer, in fine, than all that now adorn
Earth's circular board, (the table once of gods,
And whirled by angels through the void inane,)
Set deep, or surface strewn, they scattered wide,
From Hungria, to Golcond and isles Molucques,
And nightwards, to Brasil; from central Koosh,
Kumara, and the emerald mount, by Nile,
To Ceylon and Altäi; soft, pure gold
And silver, from Potosi to Yeutaw,
The angels sowed the beds of rivers with,
And serpentine and granite deep ingrained;
For boon they were to earth, and blessed of God.

Then, last of all, the animal world they framed,
Each life-infusing angel, tribe on tribe,
Higher and lower so with mediates linked
And interlapped, that all on all might pend
In mutual sustentation.
First they filled
The seas with fishy natures, which assumed
Later, Vishnoo, and mixed Oännes claimed
And glorified in memory of the first

Great form of life, anticipative, perchance,
Unconscious, of that newer birth so typed,
By signs Phœnician of divinest names;
Shark; dolphin, lover of the lyre, for more
Than one sublime adventure starred; vast whale,
The ocean beast, whose jaws, like hell's gates, once
Yawned to ingulph the recreant prophet, cast
By crew fore-fated in the ravening deep;
Ketus, and ork, and kraken; remora, apt —
Blow wind, flow tide — a ship to check, full sail;
Seahorse and seal, old ocean's flocks humane;
Sword-fish and saw-fish, sun-fish, ling and ray;
All that by coast or firth in endless shoals
Or van, or rear, heave shorewards, or the depths
Who, lonelier, haunt, and deathful; all who through
The weedy streets and gilded chambers glide,
Of submerged cities, scornfully content,
Nor wink their cold white eye; thro' marble grove
And coral copse they fan their wavy way;
Dorado, shimmering with all brilliant tints;
The wingéd swimmer of the deeps, and all
That flout the whirlpool, down whose swirling maw,
Voracious of all life, the shrieking ship
Plungeth (as into a net baited with light,
Bats); and dread Mäelstrom, navel of the main;

Dace, barbel, pike, and every fluvial fin.

Terraqueous embouchures with lizards lank,
Gluttonous, hide-winged, with horn-lidded eyes
And murderous hearts they filled, devouring death;
Monstrous and loathly reptiles, such as him
Apollo slew, Kadmus, or Æson's son,
Or Jove-born demigod, or sainted knight,
Or Perseus, on the shore by Joppa; not now
To man known, save as serpent of the sea,
Eldritch, huge, (ocean-churner called in Ind,
In Norland, Jormundgandr,) whose hoar mane
And visage sadly human, reared mast-high,
Appalls the dumb-struck mariner, as he nears
At gloaming the blue headland; those ashore
Weening they glimpse some Pharos, by its eyes;
The terror of the weald, with spiky spine;
Cayman, and alligator, crocodile,
Emblem of mystic silence and of God
(For ever blessed and worshipped be His name);
The fire-winged drake of Greek and Arab tales;
Boa and cobra, dipsas, and the snake
By red men hallowed in the western wilds,
Which nested nigh the well of waters bright,
And annual multiplies its rattling rings;

Asp, adder, basilisk; and those the Moor
Wreathes round his limbs, or in his bosom curls;
Vipers that charm the song-birds to their death
By one long glistering glance, transfixed; or those
That fascinative seek the tender breasts
Of wilful maids, and sing their souls to sleep;
Or such as him, less rare in years of yore,
Who, by Bagradas, memorable worm,
Rome's host braved singly, singly suffered siege,
Waged war, till, by arblast and catapult,
And burning darts, self-firing as they flew,
Quelled, he at last capitulates with Death;
His shining slough to swell the conqueror's pomp.

The air with birds they flocked; oracular dove,
Thrice holy in tradition from the egg,
Hid by Aturian turtle, and the flood,
To Jordan's sacred streamlet; raven false;
Night's song bird, lover of the moon; the lark
Blithe trilling in the blue, when spring's warm breeze
And pearly flowers, and brooklets bubbling clear,
And innocent sun, welcome the new-born lamb;
The vulture, all maternal, typing thus
Earth, mountain crowned, the glory of the sea,
And mother of us all; thee, bright-eyed hawk!

Soul-emblem, sunwards soaring, as to God
(Adored and honored ever be His name);
The eye-plumed bird, King Taous, who, so starred,
God's garden entered, bnt crawled out, a snake;
By winning lost; wise-sighted owl; and swan
(Sire, by the light, of Heaven's twin orbs, mis-told)
And sacred stork, thought human soul disguised;
Ibis, destroyer of sin's viperous brood;
And flamy heron; halcyon heavenly blue;
Lone contur, nighest to the star of day
Ranging, of wingéd life; the painful pelican
Self-sacrificial; cormorant; doomed dodo;
Giant-paced mooa; ostrich, feathery steed;
Bright humming-bird of gem-like plumeletage,
By western Indians living sunbeam named;
Macaw; and gold-green parrot, human-tongued,
For craft and wit predictive famed of yore;
Auk, albatross, and storm-birds of the deep;
And bittern moaning by the lonely mere;
Yea, every flying thing that wings the winds,
The rivers of the air, with spirit-like
Ubiquity in non-essential space,
The heavenly framers shaped and beautified,
For omen, augury, and song divine;
And paradisal fowl, bright bird of God,

Sole life unfiled of earth, or versed in aught
Less pure than air.
Air, too, with the insect race —
Gold-bees that boom in lilied palaces
Whose walls breathe odors; sphinges of the eve;
Moths; flutter-flies, all hued, like wingéd flowers,
On violets pasturing, their congenerate food;
And flies, which once gave title to that God
Alike mysterious in life's least of forms,
And greatest; locust; and the lamping tribes,
That light belated wanderer on his way —
The angels plenished.
With beasts four-footed, earth;
Mammoth and mastodon and deinother
(Vast as leviathan or serimnar,
In vain demolished, — on the morrow, whole);
Dreadest of brutes, whose teeth as tombstones showed,
Limbed like an oak; but all swept off by Heaven,
Creation at the flood revising; huge
Aurochs; and megatherium; elk enorme,
Whose antlers spread like oarsman's oars well plied;
These, dying, deigned not fall, but bade their tombs
Close o'er them, an' they would; such sepulture
(By glacial Lena, or Nerbuddah's banks,
Or Mississippian swamps in earth remote)

Had they, erect, and osseous monument;
Yâk, bison, ounce, and elephant, sagest beast;
Camel, and llama, costliest sacrifice
Of conquering Araucanian, who the world's
Essential spirit worships, and on whose shores
The mount of thunder, buoyant o'er the flood,
Paused, in its world-wide wanderings; beaver wise;
Bear honey-tongued, or, prowling round the pole,
Lord of the land of snow and towers of ice,
Where many a night of months the auroral arch
Broods o'er lost graves; and fox of fabled fame;
Chaste unicorn, whose generation 's known;
And stag, in saintliest legends sanctified;
Fleet-footed horse; and noble-hearted hound,
Faithful to man as to the wine-god, he
Dog of the sun, in tropic travel tried,
Now basking by the solar hearth; or hers,
Cœlestial huntress, Dian's dogs divine
Led in their leash of light; or he who guards
Orion's spacious steps; or good Dherreem,
Sung by Beyaussa, in the mighty war
Of Kouroo and Pandoo; four-footed friend
Of righteous rajah; he (that kingly kin
All vanished into bliss, and deified),
Left lone at last, shook off the shape canine,

And shone heaven's primal virtue, peer of gods;
Goat, gladly blazoned on Jove's sun-bossed shield,
Adored as Pan, or Mendes, but in name
Ashima highliest honored; zebra barred;
Tiger; lithe leopard; puma leonine;
And he whose tufted horns tree-tops o'erpeep;
Rhinoceros; river-horse; ghor; agile ape;
Baboon, too manlike, hutted in the woods,
Social, erect, club-armed, soul wanting sole;
Grim-tuskéd boar, of evil choicest type
Whom ancient myths in the heavenly north instarred
Feigning the summer sun to have o'erpowered,
And urged to death solstitial; earth, meanwhile,
The beauty of all beauties, who emerged
From water first in shelly car, wept showers
And turbid streams till thy joy-hailed return,
O light of lights; and trebly sphered reign.
All these and myriads more the angels made,
Lords of the desert's savage sands that drink
Warm reeking blood, or browse or graze the mead;
While yet they loved the earth and wrought for God
(Holy and honored alway be His name,
Sole, æviternal, universal cause);
But, ah! too soon they changed; and changed was all.

Thus made that host the world of sentient life,
With fittest forms peopling the elements;
But eagle and ox and lion, these alone
And one still nobler make, cherubic shapes,
Were of Himself devised by heaven's supreme;
Monarchal in their nature o'er all else.

With one surpassing instance all to sum
Resolved the demiurgic host, and sued,
Once more to that high end, God's promised aid.
The angels therefore by His will made man;
His upper limbs these framed, his lower those,
The chain columnal and the vital light,
Informing nebulous the limbs, which still,
Death after, lives in ghostliest symmetry,
Or fills the accustomed place; others, the flower
And constellated organs of man's brain,
Which do the interior tree of life o'ersphere;
Its nervous roots and branching arteries;
Both male and feminine, whose harmonious forms,
Conceived accordant with divinest mould,
He hallowed with His eye, and perfected
With holy approbation; to the life
Instinct wherewith they lived and felt and moved,
And all the twin-born passions of man's heart, —

That variable orb, now great with love,
And hope, now murk and mean with slavish fear, —
Adding His gift, a reasonable soul,
Whereby the good from ill they might secern,
And spiritual from intellectual aims.
These souls Himself created, for all time,
And in the stars reserved, until their day;
To each allotting its appropriate orb,
Bard, warrior, sage, king, merchant, priest, or slave.
As a free gift and guerdon for their zeal,
God (ever honored and revered be His
Name) to the formative angels gave the world
They had wrought out of darkness, and adorned
With every living miracle; and man,
As head and end of all its dignities,
In delegated royalty to rule.

Thus earth, embraced of heaven, and core of space,
Was plenished, furnished, finished; and that all
Both reasons and results of things might see
Of those creative, arbitrative now,
High in the unconditioned infinite,
God set the crowned and dominant laws of life,
In everlasting senate there to wield
The jurisdiction of the universe;

Impersonate yet abstract; and from the first,
Fixed in the super-solar skies, to all
Existence as exemplars; — being, cause,
Substance, size, quality, action, passion, mode,
Form, order, change and harmony and rest;
Duration, timeous and æterne, and space:
Motion, development, vital energy;
Will, intellect, perception, various sense;
The bounded and the infinite. Progress, there,
Majestic compensation, royal right,
Affection, instinct, reason, virtue, bliss;
Tall-sceptred law, and loin-girt liberty;
For as defect is, so is freedom; fate;
Perfection pure and death-enduring life;
The purgatorial strife, love-closed; the war
Whose end is Heaven's inviolable peace;
All summed, self-seen and sanctified, in soul,
Whose union with the unity divine
Creator and created conciliates,
Concluding all things in its boundless curve.
Night, Nature's rule, and great exception, light,
Prone gravity, and vast inertia grown
One with her seat; attraction, with the smile
Fadeless; repulse, death-destined; ill and good,
Arch-gerents of God's throne, surrounded all.

While close below the throne bright Nature, there,
Perpetual maid, perpetual mother-bride,
Sits, gladdening in her splendid offspring spread
Through starry space, indigenous to heaven;
Of seed divine, blest heirs of deity.
Angels and spirit hosts of human strain,
Bright levies of the light, in myriads massed,
All sate in silent service, till one soul,
Tuneful and luminous as a singing star,
Stepped into light, and in the immarbled ear
Of the convergent infinite, sang of God
Larklike his lone lay. Then a choir the same
In stately revolution traced, truth-taught,
Of power project through all effluxive spheres,
To the cœlestial refuse of this orb,
In a perduring emblem all the heavens
Still study with their centre-searching eyes.
For in the great progression of the whole,
An ever falling fall and rising rise,
Of men and angels, takes perpetual place,
Up even unto the pre-seraphic thrones;
For the foundations of the abysmal world
Are laid in imperfection, and the all
The purifying pain of fire divine
Must pass through, in its holy reascent

To the supreme perfection of pure cause.
For the time was when God was God alone
And nothing but God was. He then withdrew
A portion of His essence, in that space,
Girt by the infinite, the world became;
Contrast with its creator, but a point;
A point ideal child of nothingness.

These things in vision God the angels showed;
Whereat they trembled and were troubled; still
Earthwards rewinging with prospective pride,
They meditated pure delights, and reigned
In thought triumphant, independent gods.
The angels, thus, launched each on his own wild will,
Apportioned all among them, 'stablishing
In various countries variant roots of men,
Giants and dwarves and Æthiop manikins,
And pygmies; (these the tall indignant cranes,
Angered by broken treaties, drove and drowned
In sea-pools; first of victories marine:)
And those in just majestic medium made;
All somewhat diverse; all assemblant still;
Whence ray the lines and brotherhoods of man:
The sea-born seed, too, earth-born, mountain-born,

Titans and Cyclops, Gog and Magog, sons
So called of gods, Corineus, Corcoran,
And those, Hrimthursar hight, who norwards held
Frore Jotunheim, contemning gods and men;
The Anakim and Æmim of old writ,
And Og the king's sires, of Talmudic fame;
And those in sundry lands and legends known,
Whom Herakles or Rustam, or Antar,
The sainted seven, or prince of Frank romance,
By Dhami, or Durlindana, deathful brands,
Reft of their slaughterous souls and hurled to hell;
Or those who from Ierne through deep sea,
By long basaltic jetty, and pillared pier,
Whose columns, capped with crystal, thick as canes
In Javan jungle, stand, sought sure access
To Albyn's kingly clans, and fate-stoned throne;
Or those, who in Loegria, or the Lionnese
(Inundate now for ever), or on shores
Armoric, in chivalric volumes sung,
In towers of brass abode, or burnished steel,
That all the region round illumed, with throng
Of damsels dungeoned, and brave knights unhorsed,
Fire-breathing dragons guardians of their gates;
But all, in fine, by some proud paladin
Of table round, or peer imperial, quelled.

Especial spots choosing for pristine tribes,
They sank the sites of cities; after reared,
By such portentous architects as built
Louqsor, Medina Thabou, all that rests
Of hundred-palaced Thebes; the columned maze
Of either Karnak, Gallic, or of Kham;
And that once built, men say, in Arab wilds,
By great Shedad, city occult, whose walls
Towered in alternate tiers of silver and of gold;
Where bright Herat, city of roses, lights
With dome and minaret the landskip green;
Damasek old, old Byblos, or Babel;
Or Tchelminar; or Baalbek; or where Balkh,
Mother of cities, murally encrowned,
Mourns; or Thibetian L'hassa, templed seat
Of an incarnate Deity, where still
Mix Shamans and the Lama's lieges; those
Urging the stars, these, with machine-made prayers
Their transmigrative god; so shaming earth
One of the beaming brotherhood of stars,
But all alike weak in the Æternal hand;
These, by cœlestials learned, were they who piled,
Progressive from the Aleutians to the Basque,
Oracular Logan and Main ambre; these
Who, twixt the vales of salt and vulgar gold,

Not far from Guadalupe's aurifluous stream,
(Richer than rubied Oxus, azure-cliffed,)
That westward seeks gray ocean's barren brine,
Mysterious domes, in matted forests hid,
Builded; and then evanished; elsewhere, those,
Who heaped the cross-famed fire-fanes of Palenque,
And towers so high she eagles nest thereon;
Copan and Zapatero and Uwfmal;
Or vast Cholula's terraced pyramid;
Or Subtiaba's palaces, the seats,
Cities and holds of royalties unknown
(More numerous, maybe, than those named in song
Of proud Fardusi, Paradisal bard);
The unrecorded Dynasts of old days,
Who, in some holy and archaic tongue,
On altars graved high anaglyphs, and gave
Divinest meaning to each natural form;
Thus did the immortal angels, while of man
And earth forethoughtful and inspired of God
(Exalted be His name and glorified);
One city, the dark city of the dead,
Men founded for themselves, and furnished fast
With skeleton foliage of the tree of life,
And stony leaves dropped from the book of death.

But lo! all light must some time suffer eclipse;
If light and darkness freely coexist.
All power corrupts the potent, not constrained
By special grace prevenient. Thus they ceased,
Those once most virtuous angels, step by step,
Scarcely perceptible, half unconsciously,
From that pure will and primal excellence
Whereto they were connate; seeking, at first,
Their own names, to the tribes each emperor'd,
To magnify, and so become their gods;
In lieu of teaching man the one supreme
To worship, God; whom all alike were bound
To honor and adore. Through this they fell;
(No longer kind to man, whate'er to God;)
The angels fell, and drew down earth with them.

The fall is universal in all spheres,
For finite spirit, wherever tasked to keep
The counsels of divine perfection, fails.
The starry story of one primal pair,
Twin pillars to the portals of life's fane,
Or free-born deities, free as stars are fixed,
And the cœlestial serpent, sun-conceived,
Wants not, where'er is life; but whether graved
On Elohistic columns rent from rocks,

The missals of millennial patriarchs;
On palm-foil writ, or purple pulp of flowers,
Illumined with all literal loveliness;
Or virgin vellum, rose-gilded and perfumed,
Shrined in the bosom of some cloistered saint,
The same sad tale perpetually commands
The astral annals of the universe.

Nymph-haunted stream, and river deified,
Hallowed in after eld as from their hands,
Angelic and creative, risen, vain rites
Received; with lamplets studded, and with wreaths
Votive encrowned; and consecrated flowers;
While mounds of worship, sainted by the sun,
And natural altars, starwise dedicate,
Joyed in high names of generative light.
Ages of water, alternate with fire;
Chaos and æther; the invisible heavens;
Earth's æras, and the periods of pure air,
Commemorate were in terms divinely apt;
While over all ranked prëexistent speech,
Conceptive wisdom, and æternal mind.

But gradually, a separate interest
Insinuate once betwixt themselves and God,

Among each other hostile interests sprang,
And schemes of empire basely politic;
One name of God each took, or masculine
Or feminine, for deity hath both,
Begetting and conceiving and self-sprung,
Some title of divinity, unto which
None saving God had right; that so they might,
As substituted lords, the rites receive
Due to the alone Æternal; and His name
Blot from the hearts and memories of mankind.

Such were the Lord of Heaven, Baal Semim, whom
Phœnicia worshipped, and, in sequent years,
Those in the holy island of the west,
As lord of light, of fate, of wealth, of power,
Of gifts, of glories; such the father of fire,
Hephaistos, or Ifestus, whom by Nile
The wise Ægyptian honored (he who reigned
Long ages ere the cometary earth
The stars disturbed with presages of woe,
To Heaven's great family, in herself to be
Concentrate and accomplished to the death,
As in a fiery whirlpool) first of gods,
Ere yet gave time one hint of dawn; the same
Whom later Greeks named architect of heaven,

And in oracular hymns, Orphic and old,
Dictated by the sun, all-conquering hailed;
Such was the lord of waters, league-invoked,
Whose witness was the everlasting well;
Hormuzd or Ilus such, who when he had made
Espendermad, fair tutelar of earth,
Khourdad, and all the rest, her brethren bright,
The blessêd Amschaspands, and lit the stars
In the æthereal hyaline, himself
Æternal sire of light, his strength for that
One future, final, all composing strife
Saved 'gainst the lord of evil (he, of Yezd,
Prudentially still worshipped), from the world
Routed to be, and thenceforth rooted out
For evermore, with threefold thunder-fires;
Such Zeus, the living one, the saviour, hight;
Such ancient Kronos crownêd king of time,
God of the golden age, the heavenly state,
Monarch of space and all celestial orbs;
And he who, grasping loftier title still,
Styled himself Heaven, the fountain of all light;
Astarté such, the star-nymph, who in gloom
Of groves delighted, sacred where to death
She might her Hadean lord at full beweep;
Whom Asian tribes Shemiram, Mother of Heaven,

And 'mong their mingled gods the Ansarij hailed
Lady of light; she moonlike round the earth
Errant, picked up a fallen star at Tyre;
Then o'er the altar stretched her sceptral cross,
Her pre-millennial cross, thrice-hallowed sign,
Vital, and elemental, and divine,
And consecrated it; — the Dove-queen such,
Who boated o'er the ocean in the moon,
And silvered every billow as she passed;
Such Viricocha, deity of the sea,
Adored by kingly Incas, and the courts
Of solar virgins blooming; — such 'mid isles
Hid in Pacific deeps, Möooi, stretched
Full length, gigantic shorer up of earth;
High title his, sustainer of the world.

But soon in angel breasts ill passions bred:
Oppression followed rivalry, too soon
Symbols and signs of terror were, in place
Of love, God's own and holiest title, ta'en;
And the divine to finite passion changed;
Then first the primal lamb, the shepherd's joy;
Next, human victims bled; and passed the babe
Through baptism of blood and fire, to peace.
Such pre-atonement naught; whilst stormiest wars

Angel with angel waged, and god with god;
Each striving most to broaden his domain;
Propelling his adorers to invade,
Root out, and ruin all of faith opposed.
The heavens were rent with lightnings and the fields
Of interjacent space, as the high powers,
Now heated to malignity, oft closed
In thunderous conflict, till the fire-breathed hills
Grew iced with fear; and quaking, earth beneath
Reeked with the blood of brethren, brethren-slain.

The angel of the ocean-flowing Nile,
And he the heights of Lebanon who held,
And he who, where Hidekkel gulfwards darts,
Ruled with an absolute crown, for ages strove
With changeable success, and interchanged
Mishap, but each evolving changeless woe;
So too the Persian Angel and the Greek,
Contending, fanes and altars were defiled;
And myriads of belligerent worshippers,
Through vain ambition of immortals, slain.
One thing was common to all nations; woe.
Sin, vice, and luxury, with their flower-wreathed rods,
Reigned o'er the reckless nations; life on life,
Made, like that cruel tower by fair Shirauz,

Of living souls impacted, limed with blood,
Time's generations mounts of misery.

Not all, nathless, was blank; nor blight: to man
One sweet exemption, by God's grace, pertained;
One gift diviner than the angels gave,
By them o'erlooked, not all their mutual wrath
Could ruin or pervert; love, naught but love;
Parental, filial, conjugal, divine.
Life's armies were recruited still by love;
Fond hearts still grew affection, as fields corn;
Still bloomed and fruited with an inner life,
And vintage of delight; still youthful breasts,
Reciprocally fired, imparted joy,
Imported rapture; tenderest converse still,
Sweet as the whisperings of imblossomed trees,
Or the low lispings of night's silvery seas,
Lived on the lips of lovers, then as now,
By fount or mead, or wandering, moon-beguiled,
'Neath tall white cliffs, along shores shadowless.

But of all spirits who mortals most misled,
(O bold, blasphemous, legendary lie!)
Head of the angel race, prime demiurge,
Was he who o'er the wandering Hebrews swayed,

(What time from Ninus' wrath and Asshur's land,
And city — itself a realm — of Nin-Evech,
And the dæmoniac fires of the Chaldees,
Came forth the father of the faithful flock,)
Pretentious, proud, prohibiting brotherhood.

For ages this continued; till, at last,
In the divine accomplishment of times,
The mind of man (racked with immortal grief),
To which in vain philosophy had lent
Her balm Lethæan, and the ignorant hordes,
Slaves to obscurest idols or impure,
Buddhists or heathen of all faiths uncouth,
Which cloud earth's fairer half, (from Baltic bay
Tideless, and golden gap, where Frank or Lapp
With Meshech's mighty seed justly contend,
Athwart to hills of heaven, and southmost shores
Unbroken, of peninsular Malay,
Siam, Borneo, and the scattered flock
Of islets trending towards the Austral pole,)
Sought refuge in barbaric apathy: —
Men cried aloud to God.
God pitied man:
And in sublime compassion gazed below.
The eyes of the Æternal, and thine, Christ!

First, highest of all Æons, the Divine
Intelligence, met, midmost in the heavens;
And mercy to the semi-angel man
Flowed from the vision.
Men in secret prayed.
Not all that Indian sages could educe
From their Vedamic founts of knowledge rare,
Fourfold, as in the garden of delight;
Nor Konfutse, nor Gaudma, souls austere,
From Buddhist scrolls, nor Tao, son of truth;
Nor they who Zaradean rites ensued,
As after fall and flood comes final fire;
Nor they who in the city of the sun
The fateful words of Trismegist revered;
Nor they who, smit with curious care, would note,
Plucking the foliage of that fatal flower,
The oracles Sibylline, willed of God;
Whether Tiresias' daughter, Theban maid,
Or Delphic Daphne, or the sun-inspired,
By divine counsel voiced the heavenly verse;
As some in after days Virgilian leaves,
Homeric tome, or scripture sacrosanct;
Nor who from Delian shrine, or Klarian fane,
Rede sought of holiest ambiguity,
Self-guarded, two-edged, waving either way;

Nor the wise seven of Greece; nor Thracian seer,
Skilled in all lore cœlestial and arcane,
Who pierced the Hadean shades, and his bright bride,
Though serpent-stung, death seized, had half redeemed;
(Alas! not half; man's whole redemption lay
Sole, and to be, still in the breast of God;)
Nor he the white-stoled wanderer of far lands,
Who first the name of wisdom's lover claimed;
Nor he, of Hyperborean fame, who round
The world on golden arrow, white wingéd, sped;
Nor grove-priest, opening (from the ship of earth,
Or manual mound, the judgment seat of kings,
Of twice ten roods of land the base immense)
The sacred secrets of the earth and skies;
From magic or from mystic orgies, none
Could whisper to the world one saving spell
That might the house of death illume; or raise
Even in life the soul to hope and peace,
Or look for ultimate union with the light.

Nor priest, nor bard, nor mage from secret source
Or patent, Ogham, nor the ghostlier runes;
Nor rolls of birchen bark with mighty lay
Of divination, graven in branchéd signs,
Ere dim tradition; nor from tablets rich

With Auscan god-lore and augurial rites
Of volant fowl; from cane nor palm leaf drenched
With sacred scents, in gilded Pali penned;
Sungskrit, or arrowy Zend wherein the sun's
Vicarious rites were taught; nor Arian, tongue
Of Asian eld trilingual; nor, unnamed,
The foreworld's infant speech, haply entombed,
With archives of the earth's initial throne,
Below black Babel's thunder-thwarted pile;
Nor Arach, arkite city of the moon,
Whose golden crownèd ghosts shall all precede,
Kingly, at doom, though Persargadæ's graves,
Roman and Russ, or Norman's vaulted tomb
Yield up their dominant shadows to the light;
Nor where in alabastrine halls, approached
Through forms cherubic, of omnipresent wing,
As in Kouyunjik once, or in Khorsabad,
On sculptured walls, behold the king, with wine
Divining in the presence of his gods,
Mingles his arrows and accepts his fate;
Tamul, nor Devanâgari, writs divine;
Nor Himyaritic wisdom, (pointed to
Of old by patriarch Ayoob; type of man,
His seed entire, death slain, regenerate rise,)
Rock-scored, whose shadows frown o'er Sheba's sands;

Nor the symbolic meaning wrapped in stones
Snake-headed, volumed over leagues of down;
Nor earliest earth-mound, reared before all walls
By stalwarth savages, in arts of life
Less skilled than feats of death; and who, where now,
Far east and west, resurgent cities stand,
Hounded the hills; some vast and simple faith
Rudely divine, more than our chiselled creeds,
Embracing, as though fallen ripe from heaven;
Nor rifled secrets of palatial tombs
Hearted in Lydian barrows; nor could those
Sepulchral hills sodden with blood of steed,
Henchman, or immolated slave (far round
Earth heaves with tomblets, as the sea with waves)
'Mid wilds Kathaian; unprofaned as yet
By art or avarice; nor those mightier mounds
Whereon two days, from sunrise to sundown,
The warrior shepherd shall both herd and flock,
Content, depasture; underfoot, the Khan,
(God's shadow; brother, maybe, of the moon;
Sole refuge of a wretched universe,)
Sceptred, and swathed within his thin gold shroud,
Sleeps, doubtless, sound; though o'er that sacred head
Shrill sings the boor; he, striding round the base,

In meditative measurement, and round,
Twirls his long lance, contemptuous of the time;
Nor astral oracles the wise might find
On the sun's house, or mansion of the moon,
Inscribed in letters of serenest light;
From none of these dead signs came life, came hope,
To man's expectant spirit, nor relief;
The spectral mysteries of the æternal life
Were not to be explored nor excavate.

Nor Rabbin versed in Kabalistic lore,
In potent ciphers and in names of might,
Aheieh, Matzpatz, Œmeth, On, Elhai,
Aishi, and Baali, Netzah, Agla, Tzour;
Or that which faintly heired the cloud of light,
(Whence God of old by gems spake, and His truth
Responsive gleamed from every glance of fire,)
The echoing daughter of the spirit voice;
In spheral talismans and starry seals
The which on vital, vegetal, mental worlds
Do stamp their influence through the elements;
Nor who, in Babylonian gloss profound,
Taught the Ædenic mysteries of man
And maness; how in union infinite,
The fair æterne, the loveliness supreme,

The heavenly man, the tree divine of life,
Whose branches, spread invisibly through space,
Fruit but in heavenly paradise; pure cause
Of all the beauty of the universe,
And all the vital harmonies wherewith
The light investured sun is resonant,
Mates with the queen of heaven, the spouse of light,
Mistress of mysteries, and bride of life,
The golden ark of faith, the gate of God,
And temple of the king; how in this world
Man is the representative of the word,
And of the spirit maiden; in the word,
How woman typeth man, man God; in art
Of channel, chariot, fabric, and the twain
And thrice ten ways of wisdom, and the ports
Fifty of all intelligence; though skilled
To excess, who taught the alphabet of life
Angelical and sidereal and mundane,
The holy outbranchings of divinity,
And virtues of the tenfold veils of God,
Stretched from the all essential infinite,
To animastic orders and ourselves,
Earth being last of spheres, of being, man;
Not such, pride-blind, could recognize the true
Divinity to come in lowliest guise;

But for some crowned and sword-girt conqueror,
Throne-born, and in a golden cradle rocked,
Awaiting, they awaited; wait they may.

The angels would not, and man could not save.
Re-track their steps the angels would not; nor
From holiest truths eliminate the false,
And thus with God's, man's mind re-harmonize;
But as, misplaced of purpose, blent their rites
That so from mystery, mystery still might come,
And no solution, no salvation, self
Sufficing, stand within the fane of day.

Virtue and vice were preached of without end;
But as in theories of life men grew
More skilled and perfect, so in practick worse.
That vice is hateful, virtue heavenly, all
Or most confessed; but knew not whence nor why,
Nor how to shun the one, the other win.
For who of the cœlestial life could tell
As ascertained, attainable, or lovely,
To beings of nature mixed and finite powers;
And if to all, or learned or simple, free?
To many, or to few?
Not he who deemed

Water the origin of things mundane;
Not he who fire; who air; who atoms held;
Nor he who that the All, æterne, was God;
Not he who first from heaven to earth deduced
Philosophy; and then from earth to heaven
Traced the soul's path by immortality;
And, like a god disguised, died as he lived;
Nor he, the sometime slave, surnamed divine,
Rich in Ægyptian wisdom and all lore
Hellenic, who in Academus taught
The teacher of earth's conqueror, and the hearts
Of tyrant kings softened by gratitude;
Nor they who in the Porch oft dreamed aloud
Their passionless figment of humanity;
Nor he who in the Garden vainly taught
Pure pleasure as man's truest mark and end;
Whose words the very hearts corrupted they
Aimed but to purify; not he who all things scorned;
Not he who doubted all; not even they,
Manly and moderate, honest friends of truth,
Who all the tenable points of others chose
And in one system starred.

Nor better fared
The dubious mind, intent elsewhere on truth,
With the self-righteous formalist who prized

The law minutest, if Mosaic, more
Than justice or divinest charities;
Or those, who utter nothing after death
Argued, against the instinct of mankind;
And so besotted, tyrannously denied
The being of all angels, theirs except,
Michael, Gabriel, Raphael, and all else;
Or such as in ascetic penance pined
'Mid rocks, wilds, caves, their useless lives away.

Law seemed not that man needed; from the birth
Historic of all empires to that hour,
Menes and Minos, Numa and Manou;
And wise Zamolxis, legislative slave,
Who after three years death his life redeemed;
Sub-slaving to achieve his country's weal;
Zaleucus and Lycurgus and Solon,
The lights of ages, and Rome's tables twelve,
Had done what in them lay, of human force,
To better negatively man's defaults,
And social sins and civic crimes decrease;
Injustice all forbidding; but one mean,
Whereby reunion with Divinity
(Which failing, law, philosophy, and faith
Echoes of echoes were and shades of shades)

Might be accomplished, seemed unknown, unhoped.

To some in every land, of soul reborn,
The gifts of wisdom, light and peace pertained;
But who should teach the multitudinous mass;
What truths unfold, and what more fine reserve;
The wisest men were doubtful; and believed
The ultimate indifference of all deeds,
All thoughts, all motives, all intents; the best
Were erring guides; the worst were all but all.
The world was one ænigma; life appeared
A bridge of groans across a stream of tears.

Again the giant world-sphinx, winged with air,
Sun-faced, star-maned, tailed with the rolling sea,
And breasted as beseems the dam of all
Who nourisheth men and beasts, her riddle reads;
And, this time, she the knot divine propounds,
(For sage and priest confess them, both, estranged,)
Of how may God with man be reconciled?
Who solves earns well the purple; and thenceforth
With ominous and curseworthy glory wears
His gold-spiked crown. But ah! his end is woe.
He, to his fate divine, uneyes himself in vain;
His tomb is in time's chasm; and the long

Oracular thunders further quest forefend.
In every generation of his kind,
Hero, or priest, or bard, or sage, or king,
There lives but one can solve. Now all were dumb.

But now that Messianic times drew nigh,
In sweet fulfilment of cœlestial love,
Paternal, son-like, spiritual, typed
In rites Saturnian, golden-tided years;
God the most High, compassionating the state
Of wretched mortals, thus with reason blessed,
But with material nature cursed, devoid
Of guide infallible, or standard pure,
And ground beneath the crashing rivalries
Of disobedient angels, sent from heaven
His Christ, our Saviour; that He, being born
In union consubstantive with the man
Jesus, true knowledge of the Lord of Gods,
And faith in Him alone, He might retrieve
To earth's bewildered nations; and the reign
O'erthrow of angel kings who thralled the world
With their most fatal misrule; and in front,
The haughty and presumptuous spirit which claimed
Allegiance from the patriarch's house, who led
By him, from Goshen, in C'naan abode.

Allied to our mortality came Christ,
Therefore in godly wise, and humbly great;
Foretold by stars; typed by the wingéd sun;
His life one long perpetual miracle
Upon the sun-clad earth; from lip and hand
Eradiating blessings like the sun.
His words were as a well, profoundly clear,
And deeplier drawn, the purer, more of life.
Mankind with inexpressive gladness marked
His daily walk; touched his health-issuing robe,
And lived renewed; the changing dead his grave
Quitted at one appeal; sinners, their sin
Owned, were forgiven; believed, and were in heaven.

Dreading the whole defection of his state,
The angel of the Hebrews, (chosen race
As they o'erweeningly misdeemed, so taught
By their intolerant warden,) moved with wrath,
And now inspiring malice in the hearts
Of thousands, his fanatic devotees,
Bade treachery seize and slay the marvellous man.

Thousands revered and loved him; one betrayed.
(Treason most high, most base, most monstrous this,
To mar the majesty divine of Heaven!)

Burning with envy and all ill passions, born
Of man's original corruption, fixed
In fatal flesh, they bound, mocked, scourged, and slew
Jesus, the glory of earth; in that dread deed
Of human hate, fulfilling love divine;
But Christ, first Æon, the Intelligence,
Impassible, immortal, 'scaped their toils
(A fiery struggle, fatal to the foe)
By virtue of Divinity, and rose
Into the highest heavens, where now He sits,
The head of all existence, light of God.

For God deposed the angels; and consigned
To purifying penitence; their seals
Of sovereignty He all annulled, and they,
Bidden into black oblivion, cast; as since,
In mountain tarn volcanic, throne and crown,
Sceptre, and all regalia, golden gauds,
The imperial pagan of the west implunged;
In time to come, some needy fisherman,
At close of day, with his last throw perchance,
Shall joyful net a mass — may burnish yet —
Weed-webbed and foul, a despot's diadem;
But He who did the angels, calm, discrown,
Alone can give, again, their primal power.

But he and his, who held, that in that hour
Of death (hopeful and holy now) thou, Lord!
Thy bodily semblance graftedst on the frame
And face of other, to thy cross subject;
Oh! he who thus conceived thee, knew thee not,
Thy human severing from thy state divine,
Son of the living God; sole son; and sire
Of the æternity to come, thou first
And meekest of all martyrs, Christ; the crown
Of saints, the joy of angels; of all life
The glory and the blessing, fount and end;
Whose blessed blood hath whitened all the world,
And clarified creation, conquered death.

Thus, saith the spiritual legendist,
They who in Him believe and do His will,
Well willing and well doing to all men,
Shall after death ascend to Him, and see
(Leaving their bodies in the pestilent mass
Of matter, whence originally they came)
His Father's face; the God o'er all supreme.
But, on expiry, the rebellious soul
Shall other bodies enter, time by time,
Till it confess the truth and trust in Christ.

All things are intermediate; God (His name
For aye be praised and magnified) alone
Is first and last; creation circling midst.
The pre-existent life of spirit-spheres
Is that of preparation; on the earth,
Probation; after death, purgation; all
Begins, all ends, all mediates sole in God.
This purgatory everlasting is;
The fires æternal, not the punishment;
Age-lasting and life-lasting such alone;
For so long as a man hath lived in sin,
So long the spirit suffers for the sense;
So long for worst offence he may be pained;
So long his inward shadow fined with fire;
So long remorse, as with a burning wrasp
In poison steeped, shall bite his quivering heart,
Till, blanched and purified, sin's pantherine spots
Vanish in whiteness as the wool of lambs.

The virtues and all holiest sympathies,
Preponderating upwards, meet in Heaven;
And in God's bosom centre. And thus love,
The heart's deep gulf-stream, that, with warmer wave
Sun-gilded, soothes the abysses of our life,
And tempers, with its mild divinity,

The universal breath all, partly, breathe;
Hasting to compass its cœlestial end,
With a serene progression, makes us feel
In loving God the soul reseeks its source;
Being to being answering, name to name.
And every evil passion which man's soul,
With flesh engendering, fostered while in life,
Becomes, in death, a living fiend; to scourge
With patricidal and Briarean hand,
Its guilty parent, shrinking, shrieking, lost: —
But vanquished, grows an angel, bleached by fire,
Attracting to salvation in the heavens.

Now, all the ills men bear are caused by sins,
Their woes are penalties imposed by God
(All hallowed be His name and aye extolled);
And each man suffereth, on his own behalf,
What proves God's righteous judgment for offence.

O, vainly, vainly from the contrite soul,
Stabbed with the golden dagger of remorse
For sin, pours forth the penitential prayer;
Death were too cheap a pain; man's life a fine
Too trivial to appease God's proud revenge,
But for thine infinite atonement, Christ!

And it comports with reason; the less ill
Men do, less will they suffer; the more good
Men do to men on earth, the more will God
Do unto them in heaven; for He repays
Always an hundred, ofttimes, thousand fold.

Wherefore should all men purge the soul of sin,
The conscience of all criminal desire;
Concupiscence, ire, envy, hatred, sloth;
The mind of all perturbing passion; heart
Of all propensity which will not bear
Heaven's fullest, holiest light; whereof by Christ,
Immortal mediator of the world,
Man may become the blessed recipient;
And heaven be full of souls, as air of motes
Prismatic, the vivacious seed of worlds.

So with the godlike angels too, at last;
Atoning, by obedience unto God,
(O doubly blessed and trebly worshipped name,
Of all in heaven, or earth, or under earth!)
For selfish rule, inexpiable else,
And penitent exile from affairs mundane,
They, their asbestine expurgation passed,
Exalted by progression infinite,

Through conduct, aspiration, and intent
Thrice recreate, shall rise ; and round God's throne,
Where, o'er the infinite and immaculate skies,
The rainbow bends its everlasting beams,
Not drops of water, but translucent stars
Existent solely in the Æternal ray,
Wherein the spirits, glorified, of time
Coæqual with the universe abide ;
Shall they, bright guardians, stand ; like dear to God
Both man and angel kind.
And when, i' th' end,
Unnumbered times, duration unbethought,
Have passed, shall God (His name be ever blest
And sanctified) another world causate ;
The powers of all spirits shall aggrandize ;
Make them wise, happy, humble, good, content ;
In every thought, design, desire, shall reign,
And glorify Himself unboundedly ;
Into their hands all mortal destinies give,
And bid them rule and bless wherever stretch His skies.

Thus he, the legend spiritual who feigned.

A FAIRY TALE.

A FAIRY TALE.

ONCE in days of yore a little Princess, who had summers seen
Scarcely seven, and was christened by the holy name Christine,
Found herself, at eve, disporting in a fairy ring of green.

She had left the kingly castle; left her sire's and mother's side,
Left the banquet, where her brother feasted with his royal bride;
And had rambled to the forest valley, 'neath the summer moon,
Where she crossed the charméd circle, aught thereof unknowing. Soon,
Overwearied there she rested, wishing what might come to pass,

When by chance her hand alighted on a tuft of clover-grass.

This she grasped, a tiny handful: — ah! Saint Mary! what she saw! —
Mounted on their milk-white palfreys, issuing from the shady shawe,
Came the Fairies, caracolling gayly as they passed along;
Then, dismounting, closed around her in a bright and joyous throng;
Ladylings and lordlings dancing, piping, harping, full of song.
Clad in robes of silken silver, golden gossamer a few,
Decked with jewels bright as starlets, bright as berries, bright as dew;
Some in kirtle, scarf, and doublet, all of verdant forest hue.

Lovers there she saw, arm-twining, in the wild wood's shadowy slade;
There, some woful knight was kneeling at the feet of haughty maid;
Here was feasting, there was music; many a cunning prank was played.

Suddenly, the stateliest of them, he that most a monarch seemed,
(Cap of crimson his, and mantle like an emerald that beamed,)
When he spied the gentle maiden, smiling on the merry scene;
Ho! my lords and ladies! cried he, wist ye who with us hath been?
Lo! a mortal stands among us; fairer than a fairy she;
Let us speak with her a moment; questioning belongs to me.

Straight the jocund throng desisted from their pastime and their play;
While the king of all the fairies to the childling thus 'gan say:—

Lovely mortal! wilt thou, wilt thou quit with us thy childhood's bowers,
And in our enchanted Eden wander through a world of flowers?
All delights that thou hast dreamed of, gathered there shall be, and thine;
Flowers that fade not, games that end not; skies that alway mildliest shine;

Kneaded cates of amber honey, and the rosebud's dewy
wine:
Wreaths of jewels, combs of silver, beads and bracelets
all of gold,
And a diamond girdle round thee; mine I give thee
now, behold!
Bowls of rubies thou shalt sip from, and from crystal
tables dine;
And, at eve, on lily leaves, and mingled violets recline;
Wilt thou with me, sweet one, tell me! King, she answered, I am thine.
All the fairy court with rapture danced when thus they
heard her say;
Noble chieftain, child of beauty, let us haste, they cried,
away!

Seal the covenant first, quoth Oberon; and a magic cup
of wine
Straight was brought him, when the king bethought him
of the charm divine,
Which the eyes of Life had opened, to perceive their
secret line.
Deep within the rosy goblet he the fourfold leaflet
dipped,
Drank thereof, and to the damsel gave it; daintily she
sipped.

Then to horse; the gallant knighthood lift their ladies
to the sells;
Every steed was shod with silver, every bridle hung
with bells,
Like the lilies of the valley, only all of silver. Swells
Soft the moonlit air with strains aforetime never heard;
More sweet than tone of nymph or muse, or god, to both
preferred.

So they ambled on until they reached a green and
grove-crowned hill,
Which, without a gate, they entered, opening at the
monarch's will:
Then the portals closed upon her; woe is me for that
dear child,
'Mid the insubstantial regions of the fairies thus beguiled.

Streams of bubbling gold flowed round her; fountains
flung their diamond spray;
O'er the fields a pearl-dew glistened; polished loadstone
paved the way;
Trees were leafed with golden florins; daisies chimed
like silver crowns;
Musical and odorous breezes breathed across the velvet
downs.

Soon they neared the regal palace twinkling in the
aëry dyes,
Lilac, pearl, and beryl blended, of that country's sunless
skies;
While the fay-queen and her ladies, with their flower-
robed damsels fair,
Came forthright to greet her crownèd spouse, and royal
guestling there.

From the centre of the high dome swung a topaz solar
bright,
Which through all the palace darted gleams of glad and
glorious light;
Emerald lamplets ranked around it, tempered this with
cooler ray;
While, without, the welkin poured one pale and ever-
dawning day.
There the feast was flowing ever; stream-like music
ceaseless played;
There the dance was alway weaving; minstrels chant-
ing in the shade;
There for aye the chase was bounding over dale and
hill and plain,
And fair Christine on hound-high steed the foremost of
the elfin train.

Still she saddened when she minded of the simple garlands she
Wove of wild rose and of woodbine, with her playmates on the lea;
And the hazel and brown beech nut which they gathered from the tree.
What though clad in jewelled raiment, trilling, tripping, day and night,
What though plyed with queenly dainties, what though culling gold-blooms bright,
Never in the feast delicious, nor the dance's wildering whirl,
Nor the wine-cup's merry orbit, could forget that lonely girl
The ancient hall where dwelled her sire, and where, too, from her mother's side,
She one summer's eve had stolen forth into the forest wide.

Drink the dew, the fairy Fate said, that the poppy lends repose,
Mingled with the fragrant nectar chaliced in the golden rose.
Then she drank the draught Letheän from the bowl with flowerets crowned,

Flamy flowers, that all remembrance of her past existence drowned;
Thus, with lustres vainly lapsing, to perpetual childhood bound
Never moon there marked the season; sun ne'er shadowed forth the time;
Years themselves were undistinguished in that soft and listless clime.

Now where mines of gold and silver branch, in many a gleamy vein;
Through the bosom of the mountain, 'neath the many-leaguèd plain;
Where jasper and cornelian clear and alabaster pure,
And purple spars and glass-bright rocks the glittering caves immure,
She roamed; and all the virtues learned of every potent gem
Or mystic or medicinal; all gifts that unto them
Pertained, of causing love, or hate, or infinite delight,
Imperial wealth, tyrannic state, long life, and beauty bright;
These into an armlet stringing, ruby, sapphire, emerald, pearl,
Threaded on the sunny tendril of one desultory curl,
As an amulet Titania gave to her, the spell-bound girl.

Through the dwarf king's wondrous regions she with him delighted strayed;
Rings and charms and magic weapons he for her, love-smitten, made.
Blithely oft beneath the seas she roved with mermaids from their caves,
Arched with amber, pearl and ivory roofs, whose floors bright coral paves;
And oft, too, when the fairy court, for pleasure, or for pride,
Would seek the cooling streams that lave earth's plains and meadows wide,
The water spirits in their arms the darling maid would fold,
And hidden things of years to come mysteriously they told;
There she viewed in crystal vases souls of hapless wretches drowned,
Which from their pellucid prisons she with holy zeal unbound;
Upward sprang the sprites, with joyful some, and some with mournful sound.
With the sylphs in air she sported; with the golden-palaced gnome,
Earth imbosomed; or the light-elves in their rainbow-clouded home.

Oft times with the Elle-King rode she, in his chariot, o'er the main,
While his martial band, with sea-conchs, blew the war-inspiring strain;
Then upon the headlands landing, counted o'er the frosty meads,
Royal droves of great blue kine, lipping the ice-dew of weeds.

'Gainst the fairies of the fire she with tidal spirits waged
War; and earth, and air, and ocean felt how fierce the battle raged.
High she shook her shining falchion, pliant as the rushen plant,
Falchion her dwarf-lover forged her, hard and bright as adamant;
Fighting by the Elle-King's side, there she the lord of fireland slew;
All the hosts of fire were routed; crowned her queen the conquering crew;
Back to fairyland she hasted; home her train in triumph drew.

King and spouse majestic welcome gave her, on her glad return;

And a thousand tongues besought that her adventures
they might learn.
This she grants; and lo! a banquet, by unheard command, is seen,
Instantaneously furnished on the flower-embroidered
green.
On the east hand of her liege lord sat the bright, the
brave Christine;
On his west, divine Titania, night's incomparable queen;
Then the victress told Sir Oberon all she had done, and
where had been;
How from end to end of faerie she had passed, below,
above,
Scathless, by the spells the dwarf-king gave her in his
days of love;
How had dealt with Nisses, Noks, and Kobolds, Kelpies,
Norns, and Trolls;
How with Peris fared, and Shadim, Afrits, Ogres, Deevs,
and Ghouls;
She had travelled in the whirlwind; for no harm to her
might fall,
Who had talismans and virtues could enchant or vanquish all; —
How the Elle-chief's broad dominions scarred by war,
she, sad, beheld;

How with hosts of fire they fought, and how the first of
foes she quelled;
How, she said, in God she trusted; — at that word the
banquet ceased;
Shrieked and vanished all the faërie, save the king who
bade the feast.

Silent sate the maid and monarch many a moment, till,
quoth he,
Knowest thou not, unhappy child, the woe thou hast
wrought in faerie?
Know'st thou not that by the name which elfin tongue
hath never passed,
Whenso uttered, we are scattered, dust-like, by the tem-
pest's blast?
Know'st thou not that we be spirits, doomed to linger
here, unchanged,
In the sunless land of Faërie, from the light of heaven
estranged,
Till, with promise of salvation, we be blessed by holy
priest,
Or some sinless mortal give us hope to be at last re-
leased?
Till the universal judgment we, the viewless sons of
Eve,

Wander in the hollow under-world, unable to believe,
Till we hold the great assurance, for the lack whereof we grieve.
Still as we of sin were guiltless, save the sin inherited
From our mother's first trangression, ere the floods abroad were spread,
He, the great Creator, hid us in the bosom-shades of earth,
And forbade that in the sunlight ever we should journey forth.

Bounteous is He, said the maiden, of illimitable grace;
Nor would He have hid ye here, if good he meant not to your race.

Ah, alas! then, why delayeth He his merciful command?
Sighed the Fairy; sooner blossom shall the sceptre in my hand;
Saying, — in the mould he wildly struck his white and star-tipped wand.

Scarce had he the sad word uttered, when the peeled and polished rod
Bourgeoned forth in buds and blossoms, rooted in the mossy sod;

Lo! a miracle, said Christine; trust ye henceforth, too,
in God.
Rest ye sure his mercy broodeth over all the souls He
made.

We are spirits, groaned the Fairy, greatly of our end
afraid;
Though a flickering hope inspires us with belief that we
shall be
Joined, at last, with Him and heaven, in his boundless
clemencie.

Be it, said she; knew not I, nathless, so saintly your
desire;
And if mine your royal sanction to reseek my loving
sire,
He within his halls sustains, for mercy's sake, a godly
frere,
Who to pious aspirations ever lends a piteous ear;
And will grant his sacred blessing to your nation: doubt
it ne'er;
He will bless what'er loves me; for I to him was alway
dear.

Speed thee earthwards, said the sovran, speed thee,
dearest child of light.

On the instant, hosts of fairies warbling darted into sight.
Airs delicious, such as never mortal heard from human hands,
Whispered loud from golden clarions, harped on strings of silver strands,
Strains triumphant, thrilled and echoed through those dim, enchanted lands.
Speed thee, heart of love, they faltered, speed thee on thy star-taught way;
Bring to Oberon and his people hope of heaven and peace for aye.

Ah, farewell, ye good and loyal, said the princess, stepping forth;
Ne'er shall I forget your bounties, never see surpassed your worth;
If not pure enough for heaven, ye are far too pure for earth.

Towards the limits far of Faerie quick their anxious course they took,
And the hill she entered first self-opened like a magic book;
Forth she peeped, and, backward turning to bestow one farewell look,

Nothing saw she, nothing heard she, save a low and
eërie wail
With the rustle of the greenwood blending and the
sunset gale.

All was changed; and she, deep sighing, tottered on her
lonesome way,
Till she neared a stunted hamlet; children at their twi-
light play,
As she stooped to raise a withering rosebud, by the
path that lay,
Shyly tittering; thus she spake them; laugh ye at my
fresh pulled roses?
We laughed to see an old, old beldame picking up our
cast-off posies,
Said they; but she understood no word of what the
bantlings uttered;
And again they mouthed and mocked at that they said
the old crone muttered.

Soon she came where, blind with dotage, propped on
staff, an old man stood;
All his tresses white with age as with its snows a wintry
wood.
Gaffer, said she, where's the castle, that, on yonder
mountain piled,

Held the prince unpeered in honor? Late I left it, foolish child!
Mused a moment, recollecting; presently the old man smiled.

Second childhood then I fancy must at least, good dame, be thine;
I alone in all the region mind me of that lordly line;
I alone some words remember of the tongue that then was spoke,
By the noble race that here dwelt, ere they felt war's iron yoke.
King, peer, peasant, all were conquered, all uprooted at a blow;
One disastrous battle gave the country to a foreign foe;
Slain or banished all; but that 's well-nigh a hundred years ago.

Yonder castle 's crumbling ruin saw its lord, though dauntless, fall;
Dame and daughter he beheld both slain; in vain his vassals all,
In vain his son for crown and bride fought; he was left an idiot thrall.

On the evening of his bridal, souls of war, those sea-kings came,
And, ere midnight, tower and town were all engulfed in gory flame.
Save the holy chaplain, none of all that princely house remained,
And myself, the humblest menial, on the lands where once they reigned.
He, in rock-hewn hermit's cavern, life, with passion undefiled,
Wore away, in trances murmuring blessings on some wandered child,
Daughter of his lord, 't was counted, by the cursed invading host
Killed; or wiled away by fairies; howsoe'er, the child was lost.
Twenty winters since his clay from mine to earth's cold arms was given;
And so long his blessed spirit has been with the saints in Heaven.

Hold, she cried, I hear a weeping; I no longer love the light;
Back she started, and departed straightways through the deepening night.

In the hill she heard a wailing and a sobbing sad and deep;
And the crash of thousand harp-strings hands of desperation sweep;
Then she laid her down, and, praying, slept the long unmorrowing sleep.

THE END.

www.ingramcontent.com/pod-product-compliance
Lightning Source LLC
LaVergne TN
LVHW021404110826
845150LV00007B/1780

9781425512439